A FARMER

Notes from Terhune Orchards

with many good memories

Gary Mount

Gary B. Mount 1/3/2022

Selections from the *Terhune Orchards News, 1996-2021*

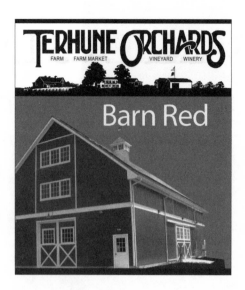

ISBN: 978-1-59152-305-5
© 2021 by Terhune Orchards

COVER: The author with one of his many tractors, this one a John Deere.
See "Tractors and the Farmers who Love Them," p. 32.
Photo by Jim Merritt

Design and production by Jim Merritt

Terhune Orchards
330 Cold Soil Rd.
Princeton, NJ 08540
609-924-2310
info@terhuneorchards.com;
https://www.terhuneorchards.com

sweetgrassbooks
an imprint of Farcountry Press

Distributed by Sweetgrass Books, P.O. Box 5630,
Helena, MT 59604; 800-821-3874, www.sweetgrassbooks.com

 Produced and printed in the United States of America

25 24 23 22 21   1 2 3 4 5

Much in life is a shared effort.
I dedicate this book to my wife, Pam,
who is the "shared" part of the stories In this book.
Together since high school, through college,
serving in the Peace Corps, traveling around the world
and taking the risk to become New Jersey farmers in the 1970s —
all these things we have done together.
It would not have been much fun alone.
I am grateful for her enthusiasm and love.

January 2, 2022

David and Tannwen,

Thank you for your nice card. We now realize that you know all about us from our newsletter—please keep us up to date on the doings of you and your family.
We have been coping with the Covid life and our farm business is doing well. Especially so in 2020 when everyone wanted to visit farms and buy their food there. I bought two new tractors at the end of that year!
It is great to have Reuwai and Tannwen with us and to see their children frequently. Mark ends his time in the army in a month and is searching for a second career. Right now he is training to be a dog handler which will lead to some type of work.

Attached is a book just published. It is a collection of stories that I have written for the Terhune Orchards News over the past 35 years. I hope that you will enjoy.

Love,

Pam and Gary

CONTENTS

A Farm Boy Goes to Princeton • 1

1996

Planting Raspberries • 3
Planting Peaches • 4
Winter Pruning: The Year begins • 6

1997

Fencing Out Deer • 7
Twilight Fruit Meetings • 8

1998

Raking Brush and Other Farm Chores • 9
Grafting Fruit Trees • 11

1999

Cherry Season: Short and Sweet • 14
The Greenhouse Waits • 15

2000

Growing Peaches: A Farmer's Challenge • 16
A Sweet Charlie by Any Other Name • 19
It's About Time • 21
Down Under: Wombats and Kangaroos • 22

2001

Water, Water (Not) Everywhere • 24
I.P.M.: It's Catching (On) • 26
Genes and Things: Growing Indian Corn • 28
Water, Water II • 30

2002

Tractors and the Farmers Who Love Them • 32
A Building of Many Names • 35
EQIP(ment): An Irrigation Story • 37
Purple Martins Return • 39

2003

Expanding the Greenhouse • 40
Sweet Apple Cider: Making the Best! • 43
With or Without the Stem? • 44
Spring Frost: The Grim Reaper • 45

2004

Starting Out with a Bang • 47
Winter Work • 48
Apple Growing, Italian Style • 50
Johnny Appleseed • 51

2005

Apple Picking • 53
Thinning Apples • 55
Zip, Slam, Bam! • 57

2006

Re-covering the Greenhouse • 60
Storing Apples • 61
Haygrove High Tunnels • 63

2007

Blueberry Blue • 64
One hundred Forty Years Old • 66
Strawberry Time • 67

2008

Farmland Preservation • 69
Weeds, Glorious Weeds • 70

2009

The New Barn • 72
The New Barn II • 73
Rambling with Farmer Gary • 75

2010

Let the Sun Shine • 76

From the Grapevine to You • 77

Casting Calls at Terhune Orchards • 79

2011

Going Buggy • 81

Learning a Crop • 83

Smoothing the Land • 84

2012

Spuds • 86

Friend and Mentor: Vernon Horn • 87

Water, Water III • 89

The Queen • 90

2013

Getting Ready • 93

Harry and Margaret • 95

What's the Weather? • 96

"Putting Up" for Winter • 99

2014

Apples: Eat 'Em or Drink 'Em • 101

Trickle Irrigation Conserves Resources • 102

2015

Weather • 104

From the Roots Up • 105

The Joy of Planting Trees • 107

2016

Our New Winery: Building a Dream • 109

Yes, No, Maybe: The Art & Science of Pruning • 110

It's the Berries • 112

Saturdays in Princeton • 114

2017

Crushing Grapes • 116

Pick, Pick, Pick • 118

Energy at Terhune: We've Got the Power! • 119

2018

Farmland Preservation II • 121

So You Want to Be a Farmer? • 123

It's for the Birds • 127

Variety: The Spice of Life • 130

2019

Oh, Deer! • 133

Winter Work II • 134

Wine Maker's Dreams • 136

Planting Apple Trees (Again) • 138

2020-2021

The Buzz About Bees • 141

Coping with Covid • 143

Terhune Stars • 145

The Great Eight • 147

APPENDIX

Honoring Gary Mount • 152

Apple Grower of the Year • 153

PREFACE

This book is a compilation of articles I've written for the *Terhune Orchards News*, published quarterly as a farm promotion for the past three decades. Located near Princeton, N.J., Terhune Orchards grows 45 different fruits and vegetables and is known for marketing direct to consumers on the farm, at farmer's markets, and via pick-your-own and farm festivals. Pam and I purchased Terhune Orchards in 1975 and have expanded the property from 55 to 250 acres in the 46 years we've owned it. We have raised three children on the farm, two of whom have joined us in the business.

Writing the many stories that make up this book has been a joy. I have tried to convey my satisfaction as a farmer and my contentment with life on a farm in New Jersey. Pam and I are so grateful to be farmers, to have wonderful and supportive customers, and to have raised our family here.

There are stories of my childhood, of growing up as a farm boy in central New Jersey in the 1940s, '50s, and '60s. Some stories focus on the intricacies and challenges of a multifaceted farm business. Others are about my professional activities off the farm. I have several favorites, including "A Farm Boy goes to Princeton," "The Queen" (about peaches), "Tractors and the Farmers Who Love Them," and "The Great Eight," about serving on New Jersey's board of agriculture.

Usually in this space the author thanks his spouse for working in his place while he attends meetings, conventions, etc. My "thank you" to Pam, my partner in business and life, is for taking the chance with me to buy a farm in 1975, when we were barely out of our 20s, had few resources, and scarcely knew what we were doing, and for her indispensable role in Terhune Orchards' subsequent success.

Finally, there is my editor, Jim Merritt, a friend and college classmate who has encouraged me throughout this endeavor.

Readers, please note that due to editing and the passage of time, these stories may differ from the original versions, and in a few cases the farming methods described may no longer be state of the art.

— GARY MOUNT

June 14, 1966: Bernard Mount congratulates his
son Gary following his graduation from Princeton.

Gary, second from left, and Princeton roommates,
Christmas party, December 1963.

A Farm Boy Goes to Princeton

I grew up on my family's farm near Princeton, and like many boys I intended to do what my father did—in my case, become a farmer. I was determined to go to an agricultural school: Rutgers or maybe Cornell. But when my father learned that my grades at Princeton High School were good enough for me to get into Princeton University, he told me I had to go there.

When I arrived on campus, thoughts of farming disappeared. Princeton encouraged us to make the most of our opportunities and to be the best in whatever career we chose, whether medicine, law, business, academics, or public service. I subscribed to this advice without thinking. I found it hard to even conceive of being a farmer — such a waste of a fabulous education! That may not have been the message the university wished to convey, but in my immature state, it's what I heard.

I plunged into Princeton. The first two years were mostly sports, girls, and drinking. In the last two years I got serious about academics. I majored in psychology and at some point decided to go on for an advanced degree. I graduated with high honors, saw my thesis published, and was accepted by the University of Virginia, whose graduate psychology program was among the best. Farming was nowhere on my horizon.

I never went to grad school. I drove to Charlottesville, and the day before I was set to register, my father died unexpectedly, at age 56. I returned to the farm to help my mother deal. The next year, Pam and I were married, and we joined the Peace Corps, a move that fit the Princeton ethos of service to others. (It also convinced Pam to marry me!)

Our three years in Micronesia led to big changes: more maturity, thoughtfulness, and understanding of what's important and what it means to find a place in the world. We were on a small island, one-half square mile in size. We served 400 people. We learned that our impact didn't have to be global to be significant. It was O.K. to be a fish in a small pond. We could make a difference to 400 people and that was enough.

1

The perspective I gained in the Peace Corps also got me thinking again about farming. After we returned to the U.S., I sold real estate for a while but didn't enjoy it. I wanted to be a farmer, but our family farm had been sold, so I started looking for one to buy. But farming in central New Jersey was a dying way or life. I was told that in Mercer County no one had purchased a farm for actual farming in 25 years. Farmers were selling their properties to developers for building subdivisions, office complexes, shopping malls — not to young couples with dreams of working the land.

We found a farm for sale and negotiated a price. It was a lot more than we could afford — we had no money and wound up borrowing, completing the purchase by maxing out on our credit card (not recommended). We were 28 years old, with one child, and starting a risky adventure.

I knew that most small businesses (and most farms) fail in the first few years. But I could tolerate the risk because I'd gone to Princeton, which allowed me to think I could do anything I set my mind to. I didn't learn to farm at Princeton — it isn't an ag school, after all — but it was there that I learned to learn.

The farm we bought was an apple and peach orchard. My father had been a fruit farmer, and I thought I'd absorbed a lot of knowledge from him, but my education in farming and running a business had just begun. In the back of my mind, again thanks to Princeton, I knew that if I failed at this I could find something else to succeed at. The first 15 to 20 years were grim financially, but I was blessed with a wife unfazed by excessive risk. With her help, I learned how to farm and how to succeed. Today our retail farm, Terhune Orchards, is a regional destination drawing hundreds of thousands of visitors a year.

I could not have become the farmer I am, and could not have created the farm we have, one treasured by our community, without the college my father insisted I attend. This farm boy is glad he went to Princeton.

1996

PLANTING RASPBERRIES

What adjectives come to mind when you hear the word "raspberry"? Red? Full? Ripe? Luscious? Sweet? Maybe so, but on this farm, others are foremost — frost tolerant, disease resistant, everbearing, and summer-bearing, for example.

At Terhune Orchards we grow two different types of raspberries — everbearing and summer bearing. Everbearing raspberries can have two crops per year. In July, the first crop of berries comes on last year's growth of canes (floricanes). In August, the second crop of berries comes on the current year's growth of canes (primocanes). Summer-bearing raspberries yield only one crop per year, from the berries on canes that grew the previous year (floricanes).

This spring I planted 1.5 acres of florican-bearing summer raspberries. The entire process began last year when Pam and I realized we never had enough raspberries to satisfy our summer pick-your-own customers. To make sure everyone got their fill, we estimated that we should at least double our production!

But, what kinds of raspberries should we plant? Selecting the right varieties to plant became the most interesting and difficult part of the project. What do our customers want to pick? What proportion of red, purple, and black raspberries should we have? How many thornless blackberries? And should we take a chance on new, potentially great varieties that haven't as yet been extensively tested in our area? Some berries may be excellent when grown in Maryland but fail in New Jersey, where winters are more severe. Or, some may be superb in New York State but fail to flourish in our hotter and more humid New Jersey summers.

To help us sort through these considerations, we contacted the Rutgers Cooperative Extension Service, which provides New Jersey fruit producers with technical expertise, testing of new varieties, and production recommendations. With the help of New Jersey small-fruit specialist Joe Fiola, we chose some well-known red

3

raspberries (Revelie and Taylor), some newer reds (Canby and CDH), and some experimental reds (Jam 2, Gel 114, and Gel 20). We also included black raspberries (Haut and Bristol), a purple raspberry (Royalty), and a thornless blackberry (Chester).

Next we prepared the fields. Since raspberries are a permanent crop, we limed the fields before planting to adjust the soil acidity. At the same time, we also installed a drip irrigation system, placing half-inch plastic tubing in each row with a tiny hole every 12 inches to release the water. Finally, each row was mounded up and covered with black plastic mulch. The mounding keeps the plants free from phytophthora (a root-rotting disease) and the black plastic keeps weeds from competing with the young berry plants for the first year. The plastic will be removed next year.

After so much preparation, planting almost seems like an afterthought. Plants are spaced between two and five feet, and the drip irrigation allows us to water the new plants right away. Unfortunately, it will take two years before the fruit of these plants will be ready for your picking containers. Until that time, we can still enjoy the luscious, red raspberries so generously provided by our existing berry patch. Happy picking!

Planting Peaches

For this farmer, winter isn't over until it's time to plant peach and apple trees. Each spring at Terhune Orchards, we plant new trees to replace 5 to 10 percent of our fruit acreage. This practice keeps our orchards young, healthy, and productive.

Once we know the type of trees we want to plant, we contact as many as ten nurseries in five states to find the variety and rootstock combinations we want. If we know this far enough in advance, the nursery can grow them to order. All fruit trees start out as a "scion variety" budded or grafted onto a rootstock. The scion usually determines the size, shape, color, flavor, and ripening time of the fruit. The rootstock usually determines the tree's size, anchorage, resistance to wetness and drought, and ability to draw water and nutrients from the soil.

Peach rootstocks are grown from peach pits planted in the spring. In late summer, the nursery staffs bud the scion variety onto the young rootstock by slipping a bud from a branch of the desired variety into a slit made in the rootstock bark. The surgery site, which is tightly tied with a rubber band, heals or "calluses" over and remains dormant until the following spring.

Once the bud begins to grow, the part of the rootstock that grows above the bud is removed. The new tree continues to grow until fall, when it once again becomes dormant. At this point, the tree is dug up and placed "bare-root" in cold, high-humidy storage. By now, the tree is between five and six feet tall and has a few small branches and a slender trunk, less than an inch in diameter.

The tree spends the winter in its temperature- and humidity-controlled storage until shipped to us in the spring. The tree we plant is actually two years old.

The nurseries ship the trees to us by April 1, the best date for our location. Any earlier and the ground is still too wet. Any later and the trees will not have established their roots before the summer heat begins.

In preparation for planting, I first mark out the orchard into rows. This is a nerve-wracking process because for some reason, a "good farmer" is defined by the straightness of his rows.

Because the trees are so small and seem lost in their spaces, I'm often tempted to plant them closer together. If I did, the trees would be overcrowded when mature. Discipline prevails, and we provide a 16-by-20-foot spot for our trees. If we plant more than 200 trees, we usually rely on a tree planter pulled by a tractor to reduce the labor involved.

To actually plant the tree, we dig a hole wide enough to accommodate the tree's roots and at the same depth as their former home in the nursery. We replace the dirt and tamp it firmly in place with our feet (thus the origin of the phrase "a plantin' foot"). Clods of dirt are broken down to prevent air spaces that might dry out and kill the roots. To avoid root burn, we hold off fertilizing the tree until later.

Finally, the tree is "headed" by cutting it back to a height of about 30 inches. We do this to encourage branching as the tree grows and to keep the roots from becoming overly stressed by a too-large top.

During the past 21 years, I've planted about 25,000 apple trees and 8,000 peach trees at Terhune Orchards. Each year, planting time is a sure sign of life on the farm — starting anew.

WINTER PRUNING: THE YEAR BEGINS

I can't believe it! In the midst of a frenetic fall harvest and marketing season, it's time to think about starting our annual farming cycle all over again. For a fruit grower, that means annual pruning. All the fruit canes, bushes, and trees we grow at Terhune Orchards require annual pruning — apples, peaches, pears, cherries, blueberries, and raspberries. Pruning removes old, broken, or diseased branches and thins out parts of the plant that compete with each other for moisture and nutrients. Pruning also develops a framework that will hold future crops and allows sunlight and air to reach all fruit-bearing surfaces.

One of the most interesting pruning jobs this year focuses on Terhune Orchards' new raspberry and blackberry plantings. Although all bramble types look somewhat the same, each has distinct growth habits. Red and purple raspberries spread through root suckering and grow upright, unbranched canes. The biggest challenge in pruning these canes is being ruthless enough to achieve a spacing of three new canes per foot of a row that is 18 inches wide. Canes that bore fruit the previous year should be removed. It has always seemed to me that I am cutting too much when I prune, but I grit my teeth and do it so we can have large, flavorful berries the following summer.

Black raspberries and thornless blackberries don't produce new canes from root suckers. Instead, new canes grow from the base of the original plant. Pruning these canes is a matter of selecting the best four or six canes per crown. The crowns should be spaced four feet apart. Since they spread at the top through branching, pruning also involves cutting back the branches 12 to 15 inches in length.

Although pruning is best done in late winter, planning and learning (or re-learning) start as soon as the harvest is completed. After this year's harvest I'll be attending meetings in New Jersey, Michigan, and New York where one of the main topics will be pruning. From previous meetings I've come to realize there are as many fruit grower as there are "right" ways to prune — everybody has his own opinion. As a version of an old farming proverb goes, "The eye of the master fattens the flock." As a farmer I've learned from listening to others but mainly from observing the results of what I've done in the field. And there's no question that careful pruning makes for a better crop. Happy Growing!

1997

FENCING OUT DEER

When I started farming 21 years ago, deer were "horrible" in northern New Jersey, "bad" in in the central part of the state, and "no problem" in the south. Now farmers statewide find it hard to live with the critters.

Since I'm not much of a shooter (either through inclination or effectiveness), I've relied on fences to keep deer at bay for the past 18 years. At first I tried electric fencing. By golly, it worked . . . for a while! Unfortunately, the deer learned to defeat the permanent electric fence, and it became less effective each year.

In the past few years I've been more successful in my never-ending deer wars. One approach is a "temporary" electric fence. The fence is temporary since the property owner from whom I rent 25 acres to grow sweet corn, pumpkins, and other crops insisted that any fence be taken down each year after the harvest. He also rents the same land to deer hunters, who pay more than I do. I was amazed by how well this combination of electric fencing/no fencing kept out the deer.

After the harvest, the fence wires are unhooked from the insulators, taped to prevent tangling, and laid on the ground. The deer run through the fields, eat the left-over pumpkins and sweet corn, and take their chances with the hunters. The following spring, as crops emerge, it takes two people about two hours to restore the fence. This system appears to be a good solution for annual crops. It seems to owe its success to the fact that each year the fence is "new" to the deer. So, for the cost of about $1,660, I've had good deer control for the past three years.

For permanent plantings such as apples, fences are needed year-round. Therefore, in our 26-acre apple orchard I put up a second type of fence — an eight-foot-high woven wire barrier. Debate about this type of barrier fence usually focuses on height. How high should it be in order to be effective? After all, deer can jump an eight-foot fence. But in my experience they just don't. This fence isn't high tech, and it does add a penitentiary look to the farm. However, at a cost of $11,754, it is permanent, low maintenance, and has been very effective in keeping out the deer — which, after all, is the main idea.

Twilight Fruit Meetings

On Thursday, May 15, the day after my 53rd birthday, Pam and I hosted a "twilight fruit meeting" at Terhune Orchards. Twilight meetings have long been an integral part of Rutgers University's Agricultural Extension Service and New Jersey's agricultural heritage.

Although many Americans know that the U.S. is a world leader in producing and exporting agricultural products, few know of the influence of agricultural extension and state experiment stations on our incredible agricultural productivity. It started with the Hatch Act in the 1940s, which mandated that every state designate a "land grant" agricultural college and agricultural experiment station. Their mission was to provide technical information and research results to farmers.

Since there are fewer farm chores in winter than in summer, we have more time to attend conferences on agricultural production, marketing, and finance. Although the need for technical information doesn't diminish during the summer, the hectic growing season means that farmers have less time to meet. This situation fostered the concept of twilight meetings — usually held in the early evening at different growers' farms around the state. At these meetings, extension specialists present timely information on growing conditions and disease or insect problems.

Prior to the May 15 meeting, I asked Ernest Christ, a retired extension fruit specialist from Hightstown, about his "twilight" experiences. During his years at Rutgers, Ernie participated in twilight fruit meetings in Bergen, Monmouth, Hunterdon, Middlesex, Mercer, Burlington, Gloucester, and Atlantic counties — as many as 35 to 40 each year. I was one of the many farmers to learn from Ernie at these meetings. His predecessor, Rutgers Professor A.J. Farley, attended some twilight meetings by taking the train from New Brunswick to Flemington, where someone in a Model T Ford picked him up and drove him to the host farm. (That, of course, was before my time.)

The twilight meeting at Terhune Orchards featured specialists in fruit growing, disease, insect and weed control, and pesticide handling. Those attending toured our newest peach, dwarf apple, blueberry, and raspberry plantings. We demonstrated our system of nets used to protect our blueberries from the birds and our new Vicon fertilizer spreader, which spreads fertilizer exactly where it's needed in the row and skips the walkways where it's not. We showed off our latest and greatest deer fence and our new agricultural-chemical handling facility where we store all pesticides used on Terhune's 225 acres and fill the sprayers.

The farmers stopped work early to attend and stayed late to enjoy the magnificent weather and camaraderie while sipping cider and eating donuts. All in all, a "fruitful" and productive twilight meeting.

1998

RAKING BRUSH AND OTHER FARM CHORES

One of the first farm jobs I had as a boy was raking brush. This time-honored task seems to be particularly reserved for the children of fruit growers and for me came just after my stint at fixing boxes. That job, which paid five cents a box, started at age ten. It consisted of repairing (or in some cases, reconstructing) one-and-one-eighth-bushel field crates used for the harvest and storage of apples and one-bushel pie boxes for lower-quality "reject" apples destined for processing into sliced apples, apple sauce, or cider. I'm not sure why my father had my brothers and me repair all those boxes over and over again — was it just to save money or to ensure our minds and bodies were fully occupied? Maybe some of both. Great was the day when I could leave behind the hundreds (thousands!) of boxes fixed and unfixed and work in the orchard raking brush.

On most apple farms, each tree is pruned every year. The cut branches fall to the ground; besides making the orchard look messy — heavens! — they get in the way of other orchard work (mowing, spraying, thinning, and picking). This sets the stage for the orchardist's son (or some other equally lucky person) to rake the branches from under the trees with a pitchfork and pile them into rows between the trees. Prior to 1955 or so, common practice was to push all of this brush out of the orchard with a bull rake — an assemblage of long wooden forks that slide along the ground in front of and pushed by a tractor. This got the brush out of the way while also removing diseased branches from the orchard. In an era before effective fungicides, this was an important method of disease control.

When Pam and I purchased Terhune Orchards in 1975, one of the gems that came with the farm was a 1939 McCormick-Deering tractor, Model O-14. (The "O" stands for orchard. It was manufactured by International Harvester.). It was fitted with a bull rake, and for several years I used it to push brush out of the orchard and into the pasture to be burned. This was always an exciting job because I would burn the brush as I worked, and if the tractor stalled at the brush pile the only way to restart it was by hand-cranking. With the pile of burning brush in back of me, it made for interesting work. (This tractor, now long retired, has become a permanent fixture at Terhune Orchards. It's the one between the chicken pen and pasture that children clamber over and pretend to drive.)

These days I take care of most of the brush by driving over it with a large and very sturdy rotary mower. The chopped-up branches then decay and return to the soil. Some pear and peach brush still need to be removed from the orchard for disease control, and I still have the bull rake in the barn. I'd be glad to show it to you sometime. Happy Farming!

GRAFTING FRUIT TREES

When Pam and I bought Terhune orchards almost 25 years ago, there were some "interesting" items that "came with" the farm. Some of the items were in the category of dead and dying. These included two tractors, one truck, three sprayers, and several sheep. Not knowing any better (and not having enough money to do any replacing even if we did) we continued to use and care for them for many years.

Some other items that "came with" the farm were in the "I've seen these before" category. They included aluminum orchard ladders and several types of apple crates. Aluminum ladders were someone's bright idea of a long-lasting, rot-proof, low-maintenance ladder for an apple orchard. Many years before, when I was a boy, my father had bought aluminum ladders for his orchard in West Windsor and came to regret it. Although made of aluminum, the ladders were surprisingly heavy, and they tended to sway two to three feet at the top after the rivets loosened a bit. Meanwhile, my father was hearing stories about growers being electrocuted when aluminum ladders they were carrying accidently touched overhead wires. He soon sold them all, and we went back to using wooden ladders. (Did you ever notice that Terhune Orchards has no overhead wires from building to building? Those electrocution stories made an impression.)

Unfortunately for Pam and me, you can't sell an item if no one wants to buy it, and there were no takers for the aluminum ladders that "came with" Terhune Orchards. So we wound up using them, at least for a while, and still have two shortened ones for chores around the barns.

Other items I had seen before included several hundred Piels beer crates bought by the previous owner from my father. (The crates had been converted into one-bushel boxes for apple picking; they were eventually replaced by 18-bushel bins.) My father had purchased the crates, but before we could use them for apples we had to remove the wooden partitions that held the beer bottles, a tough job for my father's chief crate converters — my brothers and me. The crates were held together with metal bands that cut and tore our ungloved hands. Like the rickety aluminum ladders, for lack of anything more suitable we used them here at Terhune Orchards, at least for a while.

A final category of things that "came with" the farm I call "esoteric or indefinable." One such item was a metal box about 12 inches square with a wire handle over the top, a metal pot set in the lid, and a door on the side with some old candles inside. It took me awhile to figure out that this was a grafting-wax heater — a device that fruit growers took into the orchard when grafting fruit trees. Grafts were sealed with beeswax, which the candles kept liquid until it was needed.

We did some grafting at Terhune Orchards this spring; it was interesting to participate in a process that's been practiced by fruit growers as long as fruit trees have existed. It's impossible to reproduce the same variety of fruit by planting its seed. In apples, for instance, fruit is formed each year by cross-pollination — pollen from one variety is necessary to fertilize the fruit embryo of another variety. Basic birds and bees stuff (or more accurately, flowers and bees). The resulting fruit has seeds containing the genes of both parents; the fruit produced on a tree grown from one of those seeds usually doesn't resemble either parent, and in most cases it won't be much good in terms of taste or appearance. The Johnny Appleseed of grammar school textbooks delighted in planting trees from seed. He wanted to spread the growing of apples and increase the diversity of apples grown, but most of his trees bore low-quality fruit.

To grow a tree that is identical to the parent, fruit growers and nurserymen rely on grafting, also known as budding. This process joins a particular fruit variety, called the scion, to the bottom part of a tree, called the rootstock (or simply stock). Grafting takes advantage of a fruit tree's rapid production of callus cells at the point of a cut. Callusing speeds the healing of a cut or wound on a tree. The callus cells are produced by the living layer of tree cells, called the cambium. Grafting places the cambiums of the scion and stock in touch with each other. The callus cells then grow together and interlock, forming a single plant out of the two parts.

At the farm this spring, I wanted to change one of the new apple varieties we had recently planted. This variety, Goldrush, looked O.K. when displayed by itself in the Farm Store but had disappointing sales when displayed next to Suncrisp, a similar but better-looking apple that we pick at the same time. I started by collecting scions — one-year-old shoots from the variety I wanted to replace Goldrush. These were wrapped in wet newspaper and stored in a plastic bag at 32 degrees to keep them dormant. The kind of graft I decided to use was a "cleft graft." When grafting time arrived (one week after bloom), I cut off the trunks of the two-year-old Goldrush about 24 inches above the ground, leaving one or two small "nurse limbs" below the cut; nurse limbs carry on photosynthesis until the new scions are established. I then made a split across the center of the cut-off trunk and fit two scion pieces about four inches long into either side of the split. These were cut with a wedge-shaped point at one end, which allowed the live cambium of the two parts to touch.

The final step was coating the fresh cuts to keep them from drying out. The coating I used, as you might have guessed, wasn't beeswax from the old grafting-wax heater that "came with" the farm. Like the rest of those items, beeswax has been replaced by something better — in this case, tree-wound dressing, a tarlike paste that seals for a long time, and which you don't need to keep warm before applying.

We grafted about 100 Goldrush trees. The scions are now growing, and we expect them to be bearing the new variety starting next year. If we had planted new trees, we would have had to wait four or five years before our first picking.

We have no plans to use it, but I still have the grafting-wax heater and would be happy to show it to you anytime.

1999

CHERRY SEASON: SHORT AND SWEET

When planning our new cherry orchard three years ago, I considered several factors. First in importance was controlling tree size. Until five years ago, this wasn't possible. The only cherry rootstocks available were vigorous in the extreme. The Queen Anne cherry tree on the farm when Pam, Reuwai, and I came here in 1975 was over 30 feet tall! Our tallest ladder was only 28 feet — it took two very strong men to put it up. Picking from the top of that ladder was really "exciting."

Such ladders were made from basswood, known for its strength and lightness. We bought our ladders from the Seelye Ladder Company in upstate New York. Twenty-five years ago they were still able to find tall basswood (linden) trees. Today it's almost impossible to find them. Most orchard ladders are now made of spruce, which is heavier and not as strong.

We picked Queen Annes for a few years, but the annual race with the birds usually ended up with us the losers and the birds full of ripe cherries. With such large trees, protective netting was out of the question. Hence, controlling the size of our new cherry trees was a major consideration.

About three years ago, rootstocks became available that limit a cherry tree's growth. Known as Gisela rootstocks, they were developed in Germany. Consequently, we can now plant cherry trees that are more easily covered with bird netting and short enough for picking without ladders.

Second in importance was choosing cherry varieties resistant to cracking. Unfortunately, varieties such as Bing and Ranier absorb water through the skin if a rainstorm occurs during the seven-to-ten-day period before harvest. This causes the cherries to swell rapidly, the skin to crack, and the fruit to decay. Because of this problem, most cherries in North America are grown in the desert-like climates of Washington State and British Columbia. Most of the time, the dry climate allows the cherries to get to harvest without cracking.

My friend Jake Van Westin grows 35 acres of cherries on his orchard in Penticton, British Columbia. Even though rain is infrequent there, he hires a helicopter pilot to remain on standby for the two weeks prior to his annual harvest. If it does rain, the helicopter flies slowly back and forth over Jake's orchards, blowing raindrops off the cherries to save the crop. If another shower comes along, the pilot goes right back up and repeats.

Alas, this technique doesn't make sense for our one acre of cherries. So we've planted varieties that are crack-resistant because they don't absorb much water.

As the title of this piece proclaims, cherry season is short and sweet. Each variety of cherry is ready for picking in the space of about three days. To spread out the harvest time, we've planted 11 varieties, including Ulster, Lapins, Somerset, Hedelfingen, Hudson, and Montmorency, each with a slightly different maturity date. In this way we've been able to lengthen the picking season. Keep in mind, though, that cherry season still goes by fast. If you wait until "next weekend" to pick cherries you may be too late. And, this June, toward the end of the month, picking will be "ready, set, go" because the season will be "short and sweet."

THE GREENHOUSE WAITS

The very idea of a greenhouse is a contradiction and a conundrum. I realize this every fall as I prepare our greenhouse for winter. A greenhouse has to let in lots of light while conserving heat as much as possible. It also has to be sturdy enough to withstand high winds, yet economical enough in construction, maintenance, and operating cost so a crop can be grown for a profit.

It's feasible to build and maintain a profitable greenhouse in New Jersey, where winter is relatively mild and winter-light intensity moderate. We're also fortunate that our friend Bill Roberts lives in New Jersey and works as an agricultural engineer at Rutgers

University. Bill is a nationally recognized expert in greenhouse design and operation, and through Rutgers Cooperative Extension his expertise is available to New Jersey farmers like me.

To build the best greenhouse for our needs, Bill recommended a pipe-frame structure covered with clear polyethylene. The pipe frame is anchored in concrete and covered with two layers of "poly," with a small fan inflating the space between the layers. The air space provides insulation and strength. A single layer or uninflated double layer would ripple in the wind and soon start to tear: it's only six-thousandths of an inch thick.

Gas heaters and cooling fans are built into the greenhouse. These are critical for keeping the temperature from getting too low or too high. On a cold winter's night, heater failure can lead to the loss of the crop in a few hours. Conversely, on a very sunny day in late spring, failure of the exhaust fans can cause the temperature to soar, killing a crop in less than an hour. Controls for the heaters, fans, and ventilation louvers are housed in a single unit and operate within a narrow margin for error. The unit includes a device that alerts us by phone if the temperature enters a danger zone. If we get that call, a trip to the greenhouse is mandatory — the sooner the better.

This fall we have to replace the greenhouse cover. Over time, the sun's ultraviolet rays weaken the poly, which turns cloudy so it's less able to let in light. We usually change the cover every three years. It's an exacting job we have to do on a calm day. Even a small hole in the poly can let in enough wind to rip the cover off.

We'll be doing the job soon. Our next greenhouse crops — freesia and cyclamen — are already growing. The next time you notice that the day is calm and at least 50 degrees, you'll know what's happening at Terhune Orchards.

2000

Growing Peaches: A Farmer's Challenge

Growing peaches has always been a challenge for me here at Terhune Orchards. And it's not just because the farm where I grew up had only apples. It's more than that. To explain why, I'd better start where every farmer starts — with the soil.

Our soil on Cold Soil Road has a high clay content, is somewhat acid, and doesn't drain well. The name "cold soil" dates from the 19th century, and I suspect it's a polite, farmer way of saying "wet soil." Farmers are touchy about their soil. Whenever I go to educational meetings and hear other farmers speak, they almost always say, "Our soil is a very strong soil," or "a very good soil." Never do they say, "Our soil is a poor soil."

The challenge for me is to adjust my soil conditions so our peaches will flourish. Before planting, and periodically thereafter, I add ground limestone to the soil to adjust the acidity. Peaches like a ph of 6.5 to 7.0, whereas our soil's natural ph is 5.5 to 6.0. Ph affects root function — at lower ph levels, peach roots can't absorb the nutrients a tree needs from the soil.

I improve the drainage in the peach orchard by scraping soil into long ridges and planting each row of peaches on top of a ridge. (I sometimes wonder what future archeologists will think lies under these ridges.) Excess water can drain away from the tree roots and into the lower space between rows. This makes tractor driving more difficult in wet weather, but the trees like it.

I counteract the tightness of the clay soil by planting a cover crop that gets plowed under, increasing organic matter and loosening the soil.

Another challenge has to do with sunlight. A peach tree need to be planted so its leaves and fruit get the maximum amount of direct sunlight. Take a look at our peach orchard across Cold Soil Road from the main farm. Although the trees are young, you can see they're wide and spreading. (This is especially noticeable if you compare them to our more upright apple and pear trees.) I've learned to give our peach trees space to spread out. Putting them close together may produce more peaches in the short term, but it causes the trees to grow up rather than out. A spreading tree takes longer to develop but produces bigger and more flavorful fruit. Waiting an extra year or two for first harvest calls for patience — always a challenge for me.

Fertilization and weed control are annual chores. Growing a crop depletes nutrients in the soil. I evaluate the amount I need to replace by doing a soil test; I also do a leaf analysis test to see what the trees are actually getting from the soil. Too little fertilizer leads to weak trees and small, tasteless fruit, while too much fertilizer wastes money and time and results in green, mushy peaches and overly rapid growth. I try to get it just right.

Peach tree roots are very close to the surface (in most cases less than 12 inches deep), which makes them susceptible to competition from weeds for water and nutrients. Applying a herbicide that prevents weed-seed germination allows me to reduce fertilizer by two thirds and keeps weeds from drying out the soil. Without weed control, many of our peach trees would have died during last summer's drought.

Pruning and thinning are another part of our annual care. Pruning removes broken and diseased limbs, allows sunlight to penetrate throughout the tree, and concentrates the nutrients from the roots into the remaining branches and fruit. I like the challenge of pruning. It's me telling the tree where and how I want it to grow — right or wrong, I'm in charge. But thinning is a nerve-racking challenge. A peach tree can have 30,000 fruit buds, each capable of flowering and then developing into a peach. Some buds are removed by pruning, and some of the flowers don't "set" into fruit; even so, a typical tree will still produce 2,000 to 3,000 peaches. This is way too many for peaches of good size and flavor. So starting when the peaches are about the size of cherries, we thin the trees to about 700 peaches each. This is one job I can't stand. I know it has to be done, but it's very hard for me to throw those baby peaches on the ground.

We also control for disease and insects. Diseases can disfigure peaches or cause them to rot. The diseases that attack our peach trees are fungi, which proliferate in the warm, wet conditions of a typical summer in our area. We do what we can to keep fungus from spreading by removing diseased peaches and limbs. We also spray the trees with fungicide, something I'd avoid if I could.

Controlling for fungus is straightforward and kind of boring. Controlling for insects is considerably more challenging and interesting, as well as environmentally friendly, since it doesn't involve spraying. We deal with the two insects that attack our peach trees — the oriental fruit moth and peach tree borer — by interfering with their life cycles, which progress from egg to larva (worm/borer) to adult (moth). The male moths find and mate with females by following their sexual scent, or pheromone. We confuse the males by deploying pheromone dispensers throughout the orchard. The dispensers permeate the air with the female's scent, leaving the males confused and unable to home in on a prospective mate: No mating, no eggs, no worms, no spraying.

Then there's the challenge of picking peaches at just the right time. In comparison to apples, which are picked, placed in cold storage, and then sold over a period of months, peaches don't store well and must be sold immediately after picking. We pick peaches into small boxes, sort them by hand, and put them out for sale as soon as possible. We grow many different varieties, allowing for a progression of maturity dates throughout the summer. There's an art to picking peaches because, unlike apples, a peach tree's fruit doesn't all mature at the same time. Our employees gauge a peach's readiness for picking by size, firmness, and color and will pick a tree three or four times over the course of several weeks.

I stay alert for changes in growing conditions that can slow or accelerate ripeness. Usually this isn't a problem, because most summers here in central New Jersey are dependably hazy, hot, and humid — "The Three H's." Muggy conditions can be hard on humans, but our peaches love them. And so does this farmer for the sweet, flavorful peaches they produce.

A Sweet Charlie by Any Other Name

What in the world is a Sweet Charlie? When I was a boy I had a black and white stool in the shape of a skunk that was called Sweet William, but Sweet Charlie?

One thing about fruit growing that Pam and I would like to change is the naming of varieties. As Pam says, who would want to eat an apple named Carousel? Or a peach named Contender? Or a raspberry called Prelude? You get the drift. Who comes up with these names?

Some years ago, we attended a "naming party" given by my friend Dave Meirs of Cream Ridge, N.J. Dave is a breeder of race-horses and each year is faced with the task of providing unique names for his many foals. As the mares and their colts were led out for those of us at the party to see, we wrote down a suggested name for each — Dave collected them at the end and had a supply of names that would last for a while. Of course, what we were drinking had a beneficial effect on the quality of the names. Maybe fruit growers should do something similar for new varieties.

But back to Sweet Charlie — it's a strawberry. And yes, we have planted some, about an acre, here at Terhune Orchards. Using a technique developed by the Cooperative Extension Service at Rutgers, we planted the strawberries in August 1999. After preparing the soil by liming, fertilizing, plowing, and disking, we made raised beds across the field with a trickle-irrigation tube under the surface of each row and black plastic over the top.

Raised-bed technology provides for better drainage and aeration of the soil. The black plastic warms the soil for faster and earlier growth and prevents weed competition without use of herbicides. The trickle tube waters the plants and can be used to add fertilizer if the plants need it.

We planted our strawberries quite close — awful darn close, actually, six inches apart in a double row on the plastic strips, making 17,000 plants in our one acre! Then, in October, we covered the entire acre with white floating row cover. This cover is spun polyester weighing 0.9 ounces per square yard. It "floats" on top of the plants and provides protection from severe winter cold as well as spring frosts. In addition, the warm microclimate under the covers induces earlier fruiting. The cover will be pulled back before the strawberries bloom but kept at the edge of the field for re-covering in case of a spring frost when the blossoms are out. This past winter you may have seen the white-cloth-covered field while driving down Cold Soil Road.

All of this strawberry work has resulted in an investment of about $6,500. However, the raised bed and close planting techniques "should" result in significant yield, size, and quality this spring. As Pam says, I'm a sucker for technology. But I just couldn't pass up the prospect of a successful strawberry planting in only one year. (Traditional techniques take two years.) But keep in mind the quotation marks around "should" in the previous sentence. This is the first strawberry planting at Terhune Orchards. Without the new technology, our chances for success would be slim.

And Sweet Charlie? When we chose a variety to plant, we heard that Chandler yields the largest berries and that Seneca is tops in production per acre, but that Sweet Charlie tastes best. So toward the end of May, get ready for the opening of our pick-your-own berry patch. Check our web page, watch for our newspaper ads, or call the farm. Our Sweet Charlies will be ready.

It's About Time

In today's fast-moving world, it may seem strange to think that time can be important in apple growing. After all, the apple just sits on the tree and waits to be picked, right? Well, not exactly. Starting in spring, when the apples bloom, the fruit grower must keep track of time.

Each apple variety takes a particular amount of time from bloom to harvest. Year after year, it doesn't change very much. Some of the earliest apples take only 70 days to mature, like the Lodi variety, a green cooking apple normally picked in early July. Add a bit more time and apples such as Gala (135 days) and McIntosh (140 days) are ready. Still later are Stayman Winesap and Rome Beauty (165 day), even though they flowered and started growing about the same time as the others in the spring.

Why should a fruit grower be interested in all this time? Harvesting apples is the most time-sensitive part of the yearly work of fruit growing. If picked too early, even by a few days, apples haven't started ripening and stay green and tasteless inside. If picked too late, even by a few days, the ripening is too far advanced, the apples quickly become soft, won't store well in cold storage, and definitely won't please consumers.

Apple growers use other methods to determine the right time to pick. Sample apples are cut in half and wetted with an iodine solution, which shows the starch-versus-sugar content. Half starch and half sugar is about right. Growers also use a device to measure the sugar percentage of the apple. A "brix," as the measurement is called, of 9 or 10 means the apple needs more time on the tree. A reading of 14 or 15 means it's ready for picking.

Finally, the grower physically measures the firmness of the apple flesh. While a range of 13 to 18 lbs. firmness is acceptable to the consumer, only the upper levels will store well. The lower firmness indicates the apple has had too much time on the tree and is ripening rapidly.

The true "final" measurement is to taste the apple, our oldest and most enjoyable fruit. When it's picked and ready to eat, it's about time.

DOWN UNDER: WOMBATS AND KANGAROOS

This past February, Pam and I traveled to New Zealand and Australia for three weeks as part of a group of apple growers attending the annual conference of the International Dwarf Fruit Tree Association (I.D.F.T.A.), an organization of growers, researchers, and nurseries dedicated to promoting the growing of fruit on compact or "dwarf" trees.

Visitors to Terhune Orchards have noticed that we have very few of the old 20-foot-tall apple trees left — most of our trees are planted close together and don't get more than seven feet high. I learned the techniques of growing trees this way through my association with the I.D.F.T.A. In fact, I am now its longest serving board member and chair of the research committee. The New Zealand conference marked our first meeting outside of North America and was a great success. Not only did we have participants from North America (260), including seven from New Jersey, but New Zealanders and Australians took the opportunity to attend as well. Pam and I toured orchards and nurseries, went to meetings, and even got to watch some of the America's Cup race. I was also thrilled to go aboard a replica of HMS *Endeavour*, the ship commanded by one of my heroes, Captain James Cook, in the first of his three explorations of the Pacific.

When it comes to growing apples, New Zealand's conditions are to die for: a very long growing season, moderate temperatures (not too cold in winter, nor too hot in summer), lots of intense sunlight, little rainfall but plentiful ground water, few insect and disease pests, and fertile, well-drained soils. We were jealous of all this and of the reported quality and quantity of production (1,600 to 2,000 bushels per acre). But one counterpoint to the above made us glad to be New Jersey farmers. New Zealand's population is quite small — about 4 million — and growers must export most of their crop. New Zealand is a long, costly trip from anywhere, and competition in the world market is sharp.

Part of the conference included a meeting of the Research Committee, to which the N.J. State Horticultural Society has contributed for many years. We awarded grants totaling $60,000 for research on dwarf fruit trees. One grant will benefit New Jersey's peach growers by funding research evaluating dwarf peach rootstocks imported from other countries. This is a new development in peach growing and quite exciting to the industry. At Terhune Orchards, I have planted dwarf apple trees but never dwarf peach trees.

After the conference, some 120 of us traveled through selected fruit-growing areas of Australia, starting with the island state of Tasmania and finishing in New South Wales. Our purpose wasn't to discover new techniques we could adopt for ourselves — growing conditions in Australia and the U.S. are too different. Instead, we were interested in seeing how Aussie farmers meet the particular challenges of growing in their locations.

In Tasmania, we learned that the apple industry lost the entire market for its 10-million-bushel crop when Great Britain joined the Common Market! (For our operation it would be like closing off Cold Soil Road.) In response, young Tasmanian growers are now redirecting their crops to Asian markets by replanting with sweeter varieties. We admired their enthusiasm.

Farmers in the Batlow area of the Snowy Mountains of mainland Australia grow some of the world's best apples. However, severe and frequent hailstorms threaten the profitability and viability of their crops. We were amazed at the tenacity and ingenuity of growers in erecting hail netting over large acreages.

We also learned how growers in New Zealand and Australia deal with their overpopulation of deer. We saw thousands of acres of farms where deer are fenced in and raised for meat. Venison from "down under" is shipped all over the world. Their deer were originally imported from Britain and have no natural predators — not unlike like our situation in New Jersey. Deer used to overrun their orchards. No more.

We ended our trip in Sydney. The warmth, friendliness, and dynamism of the city's population make it easy to see that this year's Olympic games couldn't be in a better place. Attending a performance in the Sydney Opera House and joining our tour group for a farewell dinner cruise in Sydney Harbor are memories we will keep forever.

And the wombats and kangaroos? Yes, they are there — in great numbers — and all that I'd read about them is true.

2001

WATER, WATER (NOT) EVERYWHERE

The drought during the summer of 1999 made a lasting impression on me. Never in my 25 years of farming did I have to watch some of my crops die due to lack of water. Each year I plan and plant with the expectation of harvesting crops later in the summer. There are lots of bad things that can happen to a crop. Too much rain, too much disease, hail, frost — not much can be done about them. But a farmer *can* do something about a lack of water — irrigate. Irrigation has made the United States the world's biggest agricultural producer and the Israeli desert bloom. But what about Cold Soil Road in central New Jersey?

My quest for more water started 23 years ago. Our life at Terhune Orchards had just begun, and I realized the new dwarf

24

apple trees I was planting would need irrigating. Their root systems were small, and they suffer in a drought. I discovered that our farm well yielded 70 gallons per minute (gpm), which is much more water than needed for the house, Farm Store, and cider mill. It's a remarkable well for this part of the state. In southern New Jersey, where aquifers are plentiful and close to the surface, it's not unusual to find wells producing 800 to 1,000 gpm. In our area, 4 to 10 gallons per minute is more usual.

We installed trickle irrigation throughout the farm and have watered our fruits and vegetables from this well for more than 20 years. But as our farm business expanded with the rental of adjacent land and the growing of more intensive crops, our water needs also increased. Watering our two acres of blueberries, for example, requires 40 gpm, and during a dry stretch they need that much for four to six hours a day, four days a week — and so on for all our crops.

Trickle irrigation is extremely efficient. It supplies water to the plants using the "drip" or "trickle" approach, with the water slowly dripping out at ground level — right where the plants need it, minimizing loss to evaporation. All plantings are monitored with moisture sensors buried in the root zone, so crops are watered only when required.

Despite the efficient system and careful monitoring, 70 gpm only goes so far. We now farm about 100 acres on Cold Soil Road, more than our well can supply in a drought. After the summer of 1999 I decided to drill another well. This decision led to quite an adventure. We drilled the well in March 2000, calling upon the Samuel Stothoff Company of Flemington to do the work. Well drillers are a funny sort. They ask only two questions — where, and how deep? You pay by the number of feet drilled, not by the number of gallons produced. On our first try we chose what seemed a "likely" spot. However, 460 feet later, our nascent well was producing only 4 gpm – enough for a house but not nearly enough for our needs. A second try was no more successful.

In the fall of that year, my friend Doug Minard, an apple grower in the Hudson Valley, visited Terhune Orchards. When I related my well story, he said, "I might be able to help you." Doug is a dowser. He asked me for two coat hangers and a wire cutter. He made two "L" shaped wires, held them in his hands pointing forward, and said he was ready to go. Now, if you've read any of my previous articles, you know I'm a great believer in science and the scientific method. Dowsing just isn't scientific. I wasn't sure what to do but remembered what I had learned long ago — if a friend wants to help you, let him. And besides, he couldn't do any worse than I had already done.

Before we went out to dowse for a well, Doug suggested he check how the wires (his divining rods) worked. Walking back and forth around the farmstead, he soon located four of my buried water lines. I knew where they were, but he didn't. My scientific convictions began to waiver.

We then went out to the orchard, where Doug located several promising drilling spots. He identified one of them as the best, and I marked it.

The story ends in December, when I called the Stothoff team back. They drilled a 500-foot well that produces a terrific amount of water. I am no longer so skeptical of dowsing. Maybe some things are not so easily explained by science. I am now working on developing an irrigation system to go with my new well — perhaps the subject of a future article.

I.P.M.: It's Catching (On)

There's a lot of I.P.M. going around these days. At Terhune Orchards we've had it for 15 years. Many of my farmer friends in New Jersey, both fruit and vegetable growers, have it. When I went to a meeting of Michigan fruit growers this winter, I found it out there. And last winter, when Pam and I toured farms in Australia and New Zealand, we saw that it had spread there, too.

I'm making I.P.M. sound bad or scary, like an agricultural disease, which it most definitely is not. Quite the opposite, in fact. I.P.M. (Integrated Pest Management) is a systematic approach for controlling crop-damaging pests (broadly defined to include diseases as well as insects). Farmers use it to evaluate a range of control methods, which they then apply selectively in a coordinated way. The methods chosen aren't necessarily the cheapest (although cost is a factor), nor the most lethal (although effectiveness is a factor), nor the easiest or safest (although safety is a huge factor). The farmer considers these three factors — cost, effectiveness, and safety — to determine how best to proceed.

American farmers haven't always thought of pests as serious threats. Years ago, when agriculture was mostly subsistence farming, they more or less accepted them, particularly if the damage was cosmetic. Damaged crops could still be eaten, or salvaged as animal food. That attitude changed when more farmers started selling their crops — consumers demand undamaged produce. Commercial farming also led to growing crops at higher densities, making it easier for pests to spread.

When chemicals — pesticides, fungicides, and herbicides — became widely available in the 1940s, they were seen as a magic bullet: one solution for every problem. Harmful effects such as a a pesticide's long persistence or harm to nontarget species weren't well understood and of little concern.

All that changed with the environmental movement. Today, I.P.M. is regarded as one of farming's most bio-rational methods for controlling crop-damaging pests and diseases. At Terhune Orchards, an I.P.M. "scout" from Rutgers Cooperative Extension visits us three or four times a week to help us determine the presence and severity of pests and disease. The scout counts the numbers of different damaging insects caught in traps placed around the farm. We aren't trying to trap the bugs to kill them, but to discover their presence and stage of development, which factors into our control strategy.

You've probably heard the expression "the worm in the apple." It refers to the larva of the codling moth. If you're a fruit grower selling apples, they can't be wormy. Years ago, growers had to spray a pesticide five times to be sure they killed the hatching codling moth larvae. At Terhune (and most other I.P.M. farms), we average daily temperatures after our I.P.M. scout first catches a codling moth to determine when the first damaging larvae will hatch.

We then know exactly when to spray. One spray does it, compared to five in the old days.

We have another neat technique for controlling apple scab, a devastating disease affecting both the tree and its fruit. The same mini-weather station used for counting degree days to combat codling moths again comes into play, this time to track rainfall, leaf wetness, and temperature during the apple season. We correlate the length of time the leaves are wet at a given temperature with the occurrence of apple scab. If apple scab is going to happen, we spray. If it's too cold for the scab to develop, or the leaves have only been wet for a short time, we don't spray. We substitute information in place of chemicals; without that information, we would have to spray on a calendar schedule to keep apple scab at bay. Many years we spray for apple scab half the number of times we did before I.P.M.

I could go on with other examples of I.P.M., but the last story I'll tell is the best. It's a technique that almost completely eliminates our need for insect sprays to protect our peaches. The two main insects that attack peaches are the Oriental fruit moth (the worm in the peach) and the peach tree borer (a wood-boring insect that gets inside a tree's bark). The system relies on how male moths find females — by following their scent through the air. We purchase tiny plastic tubes that look like the twist-ems used to close off the ends of plastic bags. They contain the synthetic scents of the female fruit moth and tree borer. These scents are the same attractants our I.P.M. scout uses to attract male moths to his traps. The difference is that we attach one twist-em to every tree throughout orchard. Sometimes I worry we're going to attract every male fruit moth and tree borer in Mercer County to our orchard! But no matter how many males find their way to us, the air is so saturated with scent, they can't distinguish the natural pheromones from the synthetic. In short, the males can't find the females. Hence, no mating, no egg laying, no hatching of worms or borers. And best of all, no need to spray. That's great, and it's part of I.P.M.

That's three ways we use I.P.M. at Terhune Orchards. If you're visiting and would like to see more, just ask.

GENES AND THINGS: GROWING INDIAN CORN

One of the things I like best about my work is that just when I'm getting complacent — thinking I know all about farming — something new comes along that puts me in my place. I am intrigued, challenged, and determined to learn all I can about it.

Every year I seem to find another new and interesting crop to grow, but this year's most interesting is one I've grown for years — "Indian" corn. That's the old-time name for it, coming from the colored varieties grown by Native Americans and ground into flour. Although mainly thought of as an ornamental, there are still people who use Indian corn for cooking. Pam and I remember the blue cornbread given to us years ago by the late Fred Fox of Princeton. Fred and his brother Donald baked it from flour ground on a bicycle-powered grinder.

Today's politically correct name is ornamental corn, but somehow Indian corn seems better. A friend who describes himself as the Indian corn champ of Pennsylvania approached me this year. He's been breeding Indian corn since he was ten years old and actually put himself through college by growing and selling it. This might seem far-fetched until you consider that a single acre can yield 15,000 ears. Multiply that by 25 to 50 cents per ear and you get the picture.

It's been difficult for my friend to continue breeding Indian corn on his family farm in Pennsylvania since he moved to New Jersey and started a job that keeps him busy eight days a week. So he and I have formed a partnership that lets him continue his breeding experiments. The next time you're here, take a look at our pumpkin patch and you'll see multiple varieties of Indian corn growing along the edges — giant, miniature, popcorn, red, multicolored, green husk, purple husk. He's been checking the corn all summer. Each variety is planted in four rows and isolated from the other varieties to prevent unwanted cross-pollination. (Unlike insect-pollinated crops like apples, peaches, and most of our other produce, corn is wind-pollinated.)

Breeding corn, especially Indian corn, is all about genes. To my surprise, I learned that yellow field corn and red Indian corn only differ by a couple of genes. My friend has been checking for genetic traits such as disease and insect resistance, husk color, ear height and size, and relative maturity date. In September he will harvest some of each variety and check the kernels for color and appearance (shiny or dull). Then he will make the final choice of what seed to save to plant again next year. Hopefully, this year's seeds will yield a better result than last year's, next year's seeds will be better than this year's, and so on.

WATER, WATER II

Anyone who knows me can attest to my passionate devotion to farming, particularly fruit growing. The fact that I'm constantly dealing with new challenges and absorbing new knowledge keeps me on my toes and in my place. It's an ongoing education about the natural world.

Over the years I've spent a lot of time thinking about water and addressing the need to expand our irrigation system. I previously described how my friend Doug Minard, a fruit grower and dowser, helped me locate a new well to irrigate crops on our main farm on Cold Soil Road.

This year, I'm revisiting our water needs at the pick-your-own apple and raspberry orchard on Van Kirk Road. Pam and I purchased this 26-acre property in 1980, five years after we started at Cold Soil Road. To irrigate the new orchard, instead of trying to drill another well, we decided to connect to Elizabethtown Water Company's main on Carter Road. We based our decision on the scarcity of good well locations in our area; we also knew that Elizabethtown's pressure was good, about 80 lbs., and that the supply was clean and plentiful. The water was a bit expensive for farming, but we didn't have to pump it or bear the cost of drilling.

Our water came through a 1,000-foot easement purchased from a neighboring property owner and was distributed around the orchard through buried plastic pipes. The water is turned on and off with a timer to feed the drip-irrigation lines. We planted the orchard in 1980 and 1981, both years with dry summers.

With the drip-irrigation system in place, we lost just five of the 10,000 trees we planted. The connection to Elizabethtown was a good investment.

Fast forward to today, 20 years later. Because of increased development in our township, Elizabethtown's water pressure at Terhune has dropped to 40 lbs., half of what it had been at the start. The price of water had also gone up dramatically.

It's easy to see where this is heading: I called my friend Doug and asked if he would come and dowse another well. He did, and together we picked out three possible spots. The next step was to call the Stothoff drilling company; when I did so, one of its staff suggested I first consult with a geologist, Matt Mulhall, to help in locating possible well sites on our property. I had just finished reading *The Map that Changed the World*, about the world's first geological map, created by an Englishman named William Smith in 1815. Talking to a geologist sounded interesting, and so it proved to be.

Matt signed on and ordered aerial photos of the farm. He also showed me geological maps marking the area's streams and known subsurface fracture lines. In our location, he explained, water is usually found in areas of fractured subsurface rock. It's very different from the sandy coastal plains of southern New Jersey, where water is found pretty much everywhere.

Matt later told me he was very discouraged when he first arrived at the farm, especially after I told him about a neighbor's lack of success in drilling for water. He pointed out known fracture lines on his map. The lines were created 350 million years ago when the European continent, which had been part of the North American landmass, pulled away, forming the Atlantic Ocean as well as fractures, or faults, throughout our area. On Matt's map all the fracture lines run parallel, northeast to southwest. Most of the streams run in the same direction, often right over a fracture line.

It didn't appear that any fractures crossed the farm, however. But when Matt and I walked around the property, something became apparent about our two distinct soil types. The line of separation between the red-shale and gray-clay soils, when mapped out, ran northeast to southwest. The line represented a subsurface fracture zone and a chance for finding water. Before he left that day, Matt and I marked out two likely spots for drilling.

I now faced a dilemma: none of the dowser's spots and the geologist's spots were anywhere near each other. Despite my scientific leaning, I couldn't ignore the success I'd had last year based on the advice of Doug the dowser. So the first drilling attempt would be at one of his sites. I called the Stothoffs (the firm is run by brothers), who sent driller Jim Kintzel to our place. After Jim set up his equipment and started drilling, I waited anxiously. After drilling 400 feet without finding water, he stopped.

I was eager to try again. After all, the second try had succeeded at our farm on Cold Soil Road. This time we picked one of the geologist's sites. Jim got set up to start the next day. By the time I arrived that morning, he'd been drilling for several hours, and I could tell what was happening from a long ways away: Jim and his helper were wearing rain suits. It wasn't raining, but I could see water shooting from the ground — they'd struck a well! The Elizabethtown Water Company's low pressure and high prices would bother me no more.

The Stothoffs say I'm a lucky guy to find two good wells in our area. I agree, but not for that reason. I'm lucky to be a farmer, a vocation that challenges me, demands my full attention, and always teaches me new and interesting things.

2002

TRACTORS AND THE FARMERS WHO LOVE THEM

My father once asked my grandfather, whose farm was in West Windsor, what he and his farmer friends talked about whenever they got together. His answer: "Horses and women." In my father's day, it was probably, "Tractors and women."

An enduring theme of farm life has been the farmer's relationship with his horses and tractors. One of my uncles sketched a map of my grandfather's farm as it looked circa 1910. It shows the horse barn and lists all of the horses he could remember by name — Tom, Dan, Jumbo, Dick, Pansy, Ned, Charlie, Lester, Stewart, John,

Bonehead, and Jenny. They did the plowing, planting, cultivating, haying, harvesting, hauling, and transporting of people. Horses were also used for pulling ropes that hoisted hay into the top of the barns and for powering various pieces of stationary equipment.

In 1916, my grandfather William M. Mount bought his first tractor, an Avery Model 8-16. The number 8 meant the tractor could exert the same pull as eight horses (i.e., eight horsepower). The larger number (16) was the power of the engine — almost half its power was lost in the transmission and gears! Gears were shifted by a hand lever that moved the entire engine assembly forward and back to engage the correct gear combinations. The tractor was powered by kerosene and used gasoline to start it. Along with the two fuel tanks, a third tank held water, which was added in small amounts to the kerosene to suppress combustion knocking (pinging), and to increase power.

In short order, my grandfather bought two more Avery tractors, a 6-12 and a 12-25. He liked them so much that he became an Avery tractor dealer. His four sons, including my father, had the job of delivering them. No driver's license was needed in those days, and the steel-wheeled behemoths were driven along the road to their destination. My father and his brothers returned to the farm "by shanks-mare" (on foot).

The first tractors were large and heavy and difficult to maneuver, and they had cleated steel wheels that jarred the operator to his bones. But everything considered, farmers preferred them to horses. They had greater pulling power, and every tractor had a powered pulley that could drive a flat-belt. The belt was attached to a piece of machinery such as a thresher or circular saw. I have actually used a saw powered by a belt from one of my father's tractors. Luckily, I survived with all limbs intact.

As tractors on farms increased, they became more powerful and easier to use, and rubber tires replaced steel. My father and one of his brothers argued whether steel or rubber pulled better. To settle the matter, they hooked two of my grandfather's tractors together, back-to-back, and drove them forward as hard as they could in a tractor tug-of-war. It was a dead heat — the tractors didn't budge but just sat there, churning holes in the ground. It didn't please my grandfather.

The advent of rubber tires led to the Avery Company's demise. My grandfather switched to selling Case tractors while retaining the same delivery staff (my father and uncles).

When I grew up, there was only one tractor to have on the farm — Case. However, when I was ten, my father bought a Ferguson — a radical step, although the Ferguson had features that made it more suitable than Case for some farm jobs.

Just as they were with horses, farmers are particular about their tractors. Even today, many rural towns divide farmers according to their tractors. You'll hear people say, "He's a John Deere man," or "He's a Case man." Sometimes they'll substitute a tractor's color for its manufacturer. Just last week someone told me, "They're all green over there," meaning they all drive John Deere tractors.

No farmer is lukewarm about his tractors. Several years ago I traveled to Biglerville, Pa., to buy a new sprayer for our orchards. The dealer took me to see a particular model on someone's farm. When I asked the farmer how he liked the sprayer, he said sternly, "It works good, but only if you have something green to put in front of it." It wasn't clear he would even let me look at the sprayer if I wasn't going to pull it with a John Deere. Something red (Case or International), orange (Allis Chalmers), or blue (Ford) just wouldn't do.

So you really can't separate farmers and their tractors. For any self-respecting farmer, it's a case of the more the better. This statement doesn't necessarily hold for the farmer's spouse, however. One year just before Thanksgiving dinner at our house, my younger brother Tim walked around the farmstead, just looking things over. At dinner, between mouthfuls of turkey, he asked, "Gary, why do you need 13 tractors?" The dead silence that followed was broken by Pam's question: "We . . . have . . . 13 . . . tractors?" Which is why farmers never, ever park all of their tractors in a row — too easy to count!

As I write this, I'm thinking about getting a new tractor. It's something I desperately need.

* *

My thanks to brothers Bill and Lee for help for this article.

A Building of Many Names

The Terhune Orchards Farm Store has always engaged my interest — its architecture, function, history, and the names it's been known by over time. In our early years of owning Terhune Orchards we called it the "apple building." I recently talked with Richard (Dick) Terhune, a member of the Terhune family that sold us the farm 28 years ago. He told me his family always called it the apple *house*, as in farmhouse, cider house, smokehouse, wash house, etc. In his day, apples were the main crop, although the family also grew some peaches. We now grow some 32 different crops, all sold at what we now call the farm *store*.

The farm-store building was constructed in the 1930s. The Terhunes dug the basement with a "bull scoop" pulled by a Fordson tractor. (They were called this because when Henry Ford first started selling tractors, the name Ford was already taken by another manufacturer. So he formed a new company, Henry Ford & Son, and named the tractors Fordson.) The scoop had two handles, similar to wheelbarrow handles, manipulated by an operator who walked behind it. As the tractor pulled the scoop along, the operator pushed the handles up to scrape off a layer of soil. At the end of a run, the tractor pulled the scoop up a ramp and the operator lifted the handles sharply, dumping the contents. Tractor, scoop, and operator made many passes, scooping up a bit of earth each time.

Dick related a family story about the scoop uncovering a spring during the basement's excavation. The family was relieved that the tractor had been parked up and out of the basement for the night because by morning it was filled with water! To this day, the spring runs through the basement and fills the small pond behind the store.

Apples were stored in the basement, fruit was sorted and packed on the main floor, and empty boxes and baskets were stored in the attic. Dick's sister, Elsie Terhune Davison, told me that she and her sister Ruth liked to roller-skate on the main floor in the off-season. According to Elsie, Ruth was the better skater.

All the apples were picked and stored in half-bushel baskets — similar to the baskets used to display apples in the Farm Store today. The baskets were open at the top and stacked pyramid-style on the basement floor. This took some skill, as I found out when I tried it.

Cooling the stored apples was accomplished by means of cellar doors and an air tunnel that went all the way up to the cupola on top of the building. The doors were kept open day and night; cool air came in through the doors and hot air rose up through the air tunnel and out the cupola. The doors were closed only when outdoor temperatures dropped low enough to freeze and spoil the apples. The running spring also helped cool the air and keep the humidity high. Apples kept well in this storage, often into January. In the 1960s, the family installed a refrigeration unit.

In Dick and Elsie's day, apples were lifted by hand through a trap door to the main floor. Today, all apple containers are handled with a forklift, but it was several years after our purchase of Terhune Orchards in 1975 before we could afford such a labor-saving machine.

I've always wondered about the building's design. Dick and Elsie related how their father, the builder of the apple house, worked closely with what was always referred to as "the college." (Older New Jersey farmers refer to Rutgers' Cook College this way, I suppose because of its former name, the College of Agriculture.) His close association with the college and the building's functionality suggest that agricultural engineers — perhaps from the "college" — were involved in the design.

The first electricity in the apple house was direct current supplied by storage batteries kept in an old smokehouse, located between the apple house and farmhouse. The batteries were charged by a wind-powered Delco generator mounted on the windmill next to the farmhouse. (Unfortunately, neither the windmill nor the smokehouse exists today.) The main use of electric power was for lighting, and wires were also run to the barn and farmhouse. Elsie recalls that the system powered their first electric clothes washer, which they had to re-wire after the farm connected to the grid and its alternating current. The family joked that when low batteries caused the lights to dim, it was time for bed.

In 1978, Pam and I added a front porch to the Farm Store, followed later by a rear addition for preparing fruits and vegetables for sale.

Pam and I love the Farm Store. The interior has undergone many changes — new walls, additional windows, a higher ceiling, and new floor. We covered the walls with old farm tools from my grandfather's farm. During the busiest times of the year the store is too small, but most of the time it's just right.

Writing all this reminds me how different farm life was a century ago. Many fewer people lived in this part of New Jersey, and families were often connected in ways now forgotten. Dick Terhune had a big surprise for me when I talked to him about the apple house. He told me that his grandfather, the first Terhune to own this farm, was named Richard *Mount* Terhune. I put my brother Lee Mount, the family genealogist, on the case. Lee found that Richard Mount Terhune's mother's maiden name was Mary A. Mount. Also that his mother-in-law's maiden name was Edna E. Mount. Both women shared common ancestors with my father's family.

When Pam and I bought the farm back in 1975, we had no idea it was a family affair.

* *

My thanks for help on this story to members of the greater Terhune family: Dick Terhune, Elsie Terhune Davison, Charles Hunt (Dick and Elsie's brother-in-law), and my brother Lee.

EQIP(MENT): AN IRRIGATION STORY

I've said it before — each time I think that I know what I'm doing in farming, something new and unexpected comes along to surprise me.

The 2002 growing season is bringing new challenges for farmers in our area. By this I mean the drought. Many New Jersey farmers are wondering if we're facing another summer like that of 1999, one of the driest ever. For me, 1999 served as a wake-up call. It made me realize that I had better be ready to adequately water my crops — and to do so with the smallest amount of water possible.

For a farmer, the problems of drought are self-evident — no water equals no crops and no income. Drought compounds the problems for fruit growers. It reduces the number of fruit a tree produces as well as their size and quality. Most fruit-bearing trees and plants develop flower buds for next year at the same time that they're growing fruit for the current year, so a drought can impact a crop over several years. In areas of low rainfall and sandy soil, a drought can actually kill fruit trees. Although my front lawn at the farm may turn brown and look dead during a drought, it's really just dormant and comes back when it rains. Not so with fruit trees.

In 1980, Pam and I purchased a farm on Van Kirk Road and planted apples and raspberries. That's where we now have our pick-your-own orchards. I installed trickle irrigation there, and as a result the orchards have been watered very efficiently over the years. Drip irrigation delivers water slowly and in small amounts, right at ground level. Little is lost to evaporation or runoff. My trees and raspberries have survived several dry years.

In the 1980s my irrigation system was state of the art. But that was a while ago, and after the drought of 1999 I started thinking about how I could improve my system. Maybe there were better ways to water trees and use water more efficiently. And while I hated to admit the possibility, maybe there were people out there who knew more about irrigation than I did.

Recently I've been working with a federal-state conservation initiative, known as EQIP (Environmental Quality Incentives Program), designed to improve the environmental quality of farming enterprises. The program made experts available to advise me on my plans to rehabilitate my irrigation system on Van Kirk Road. I wound up installing new piping to deliver water to each section of the orchard, new control valves in each section, and modern tubing that releases water evenly throughout each row. These improvements have made a tremendous difference. I run the system about half as long as I did before, and I don't have to over-water trees at the beginning of a row to ensure that trees at the end of the row get the water they need. Buried sensors tell me exactly when the soil is moist enough.

As I've said before, every time I think I know what I'm doing, something new comes along to remind me I don't.

PURPLE MARTINS RETURN

Four or five years ago, I was surprised to receive a purple martin house as a birthday present from my family. I love purple martins; they are migratory birds with some of the most interesting habits of any birds.

Purple martin houses are literally apartment houses for birds. Purple martins live in colonies and almost exclusively in housing built for them by humans. Native Americans were making martin houses from hollow gourds, and hanging them near their homesites, long before the arrival of European explorers.

Martin houses can be sets of "single family" dwellings hung near each other or "multifamily" units with 10, 20, or more attached dwellings. They are mounted on poles about 15 feet off the ground.

I've been interested in purple martins for a long time, starting with my first martin house at my parents' home near Grovers Mill. Years later, shortly after Pam and I bought Terhune Orchards, my brother Bill built us a martin house.

Neither of these martin houses were successful in attracting martins, but I was determined to do better with the house my family gave me as a birthday present. It seems that the biggest factor in attracting martins conforms to the old real-estate maxim: location, location, location. Martins don't like living near trees — they feed on flying insects and need airspace to swoop and dive on their prey. They don't like undergrowth near the base of the pole, where too many predators such as raccoons or snakes can hide, ready to climb the pole at night. Martins do like places with a good food supply — near a pond, for instance.

I was surprised to learn that purple martins also like living near people. It's as though they enjoy having an audience for their aerial show of catching every flying insect in sight. So I made sure to place my new "low income housing" as close as possible to our farm buildings.

Purple martins spend their winters far south, in Brazil. They migrate north, with the first ones arriving in the southern U.S. — Texas or Louisiana — in February or March; they reach our area about April 1. The first ones to make their appearance are adult males, so black in color they're almost purple. They check out the accommodations and, if they approve, hang around waiting for the rest of the family to arrive. Early each morning, they soar high above the farm singing their dawn song.

One theory suggests that arriving females and young adults hear the song and are attracted to the site. The martins move in, sometimes evicting local squatters such as sparrows. They raise a family and are with us all summer, filling the air with their twangy chirping, recognized immediately by any martin enthusiast. In mid-August they depart on their long journey south.

My first year, I didn't get my new martin house put up soon enough. I had to put it together, which took some time — so many little parts! — so it wasn't ready for occupancy until Memorial Day. To my surprise, martins showed up three days later. They were young adults, probably escaping crowded conditions elsewhere. Although the martins set up housekeeping, they were unsuccessful in raising a family. Still, it was great having them around, and each year since we've been lucky to have several families visit for the summer. I've put up another apartment house and several fiberglass gourds as well. As I write this while returning from an Easter visit to our daughter Tannwen in San Francisco, I wonder who will get home first — Pam and me or the martins.

Please join us in enjoying the purple martins. You can watch the fun through the telescope we set up on the Farm Store porch or from a nearby picnic table. For additional information, visit www.purplemartin.org.

2003

EXPANDING THE GREENHOUSE

This year we're expanding our greenhouse at Terhune Orchards. We first built the greenhouse 12 years ago. Prior to that, we hadn't grown very many of the plants we sold. Mostly we bought them from other farmers for resale. But growing our own plants, in our own greenhouse, gives us the flexibility to grow exactly the varieties we want, either for selling or for transplanting to our fields. They're better-quality plants, and most of all, growing them is more fun.

Our original greenhouse was 50 by 48 feet, just under 2,500 square feet. It quickly became too small for Pam, the green thumb of the family. There are just so many nice things to grow! This year we're doubling the size to 50 by 96 feet — nearly 5,000 square feet.

Our growing season begins with freesia; we make successive plantings of this bulb, starting in September. They're the most fantastic plants, with long stems and multiple flowers lined up in a row, hanging off the top. Freesias originated in South America and aren't widely grown in New Jersey. Many nursery greenhouses are full of poinsettias in the fall, with no room left to plant freesias. Pam and I have never cared about growing poinsettias, so we have room. Freesias also take a long time to grow. The first ones are ready to sell in January.

Along with freesia, we plant primrose and cyclamen — transported to the Farm Store for sale as they mature. At the same time, we also plant tulips, daffodils, tête-à-tête, and grape hyacinth. Before we plant any of these bulbs, however, they take a side trip to the bulb cooler for a few months. The bulb cooler is a completely dark and refrigerated room. Those conditions allow the bulb roots to develop, but the cold temperature and the darkness keep the tops from growing. After two or three months, the roots have filled the pots, but the tops are only two inches tall and without any green color. Starting in January, we bring a few out into the greenhouse each week. After two weeks, they have grown, turned green, started to flower, and are ready to sell. Fantastic!

One reason I like greenhouse growing so much is that I get to control the weather — at least the inside weather. Heaters, powered by natural gas, maintain a constant temperature. Fans cool the greenhouse when the sun is shining. Each plant gets the exact amount of water it needs and, by adding insect screening and grow-lights (to extend the growing day), we can further control the environment.

It stays warm in the greenhouse all winter. Here at the farm, where we work outside 12 months of the year, Pam never has trouble finding people to help her inside the greenhouse. On a cold day it rates right up there with the bakery as a nice place to be.

After all the winter bulbs have flowered and sold, we start growing our spring flowers and herbs and the vegetable plants we will transplant into the fields — tomatoes, peppers, eggplant, squash, watermelon, cantaloupe, and in summer, broccoli, collards, and brussel sprouts.

Some plants arrive as "plugs." They are already-germinated seeds, a half-inch high. These tiny plants come 72, 144, 225, or more to a 10-by-20-inch flat. We transplant them to pots or hanging baskets, then put them in the greenhouse to grow. We grow other plants from seed. We first sow the seeds in rows in a fine-textured soil mix and place the sowing tray on a heated bench. We mist the bench frequently and transplant the tiny plants to pots when they get about three-quarters of an inch tall.

All in all, it's a complicated process. Every variety has its particular needs and grows at its own pace, and getting the best results requires a lot of patience and attention to detail. Making it all come out right is deeply satisfying.

Then, there's the technology of greenhouses. As Pam says, I'm a sucker for technology. One of the best examples is the greenhouse monitor. If it gets too cold, too hot, or if the electricity goes off, the monitor calls me up immediately. I pick up the phone and hear the recording, "The temperature is too low." That means it's time for me to get out there and fix the heaters. If I'm not home, the machine calls three other people in sequence. On a cold night, greenhouse temperatures can fall to damaging levels in as little as four or five hours. Or on a hot day, without the cooling fans, the temperature can soar to plant-killing levels in as little as an hour. This past Christmas, while I was on vacation, the electricity went off during a snowstorm. Fortunately, the machine summoned two key employees who came in and started a generator to power the heaters.

My latest greenhouse technology is a generator that kicks on automatically if power goes off. In runs off our natural-gas line (no fuel tank to go empty, no gasoline to turn stale) and starts, comes to full power, and switches over in 20 seconds after a power outage. It runs until power is restored, whether that takes hours or days. The generator has a timer that starts it up once a week and test-runs it for 20 minutes.

Along with electricity failures and temperature extremes inside the greenhouse, I worry about snow. Whenever it snows, I have to turn the heat way up so the flakes melt as soon as they hit the greenhouse roof. Letting snow accumulate can collapse the roof or lead to the formation of ice, which if blown by wind can slice the greenhouse plastic to ribbons. I worry about hailstorms, too — a severe one like we had in June of this year can puncture holes in the plastic, which we would then have to replace.

Mostly, the greenhouse is an enjoyable challenge. It gives me a chance to control the inside weather, has a lot of neat, complicated devices to occupy me, and provides brightness and warmth during long New Jersey winters.

Sweet Apple Cider: Making the Best!

I've come full circle in my attempts to make the best apple cider possible. Make that two full circles. Ideas I tried early on, then abandoned, then tried again in a different way, are now either back in or back out. As I've found over the years, there's more than one way to make apple cider. But you'll be all right so long as you keep to the basics.

Start with sound, ripe apples. Don't use just one variety, but a blend of different types. By sound apples I mean ones that are healthy and appealing to the eye: no decay, no major bruises. I tell my cider makers, "If you see an apple you wouldn't eat, don't put it in the cider press."

Cider apples, like eating apples, should be at peak ripeness. You can't make good cider using immature apples. In a ripe (mature) apple, the starches have mostly changed to sugars. Eating an immature, starchy apple evokes adjectives like woody, tasteless, green, or mealy.

Keep your equipment spotlessly clean. It's a lot of work. If you're making a batch of just four or five hundred gallons, cleaning up afterward can take more time than pressing the cider in the first place. Items to be cleaned: bin dumper, sorting rollers, apple washer, bucket elevator, apple grinder, pomace tank, pomace pump, cider press, press cloths, cider pumps, cider filter, storage tanks, pasteurizer, jug filler. For most items, a pressure wash at 1,000 psi does the trick.

Cool cider immediately after pressing and pasteurizing. Each of our 400-gallon storage tanks has its own 2-horsepower cooling system. The best cider is made without preservatives. At warm temperatures, fermentation starts quickly, and refrigeration (as close to 32 degrees as possible) is key to preventing it.

As for the actual blend of varieties, every cider maker has a preference. The exact mix usually changes over the season and isn't often divulged. It's like asking a Maine lobsterman where he catches his lobsters. *Ey-yup!*

The more I learn about making cider, the more I realize how much the basics count. I keep trying new ways to refine the basics. This year, for example, we will debut a plan for cider quality and safety. We've worked it out in conjunction with the U.S. Food and Drug Administration and the N.J. Department of Health at a seminar sponsored by the New Jersey Horticultural Society, of which I'm treasurer. Our plan should go a long way toward keeping Terhune cider the very best.

WITH OR WITHOUT THE STEM?

Here at Terhune Orchards we offer customers the option of picking their own fruit. Depending on season, they can choose between pick-your-own strawberries, blueberries, raspberries, peaches, apples, and cherries. For cherries, the weightiest question is whether to pick them with or without the stem. There are advantages and disadvantages to each. It's easier and faster to pick them without the stem, but depending on how you're planning to consume your cherries, this isn't necessarily the best method.

Cherry stems are two to three inches long. At bloom, the flower clusters are tight to the limb. Once a flower is pollinated the stem grows rapidly, giving the developing cherry room to grow. This is critical, for if packed too close together cherries can become deformed and are also susceptible to decay from excessive moisture.

Regardless of how you pick them, you won't run out of cherries — we have them in abundance. I read about a contest in Washington State to guess the number of cherries on a tree. When someone actually counted them, the correct answer turned out to be 12,999! The tree was probably larger than any of ours (we plant dwarf varieties for easy picking). Still, two acres times 300 trees per acre times whatever number of cherries per tree equals . . . lots of cherries.

Our cherries don't all have to be picked at the same time, however. We have 11 varieties of sweet cherries: Hudson, Somerset, Ulster, Heidelfingen, Lapins, Van, Sam, Ranier, Hartland, Chelan, and Schmidt, as well as Montmorency sour cherries. Each variety ripens at a slightly different point in the season, so the harvest can be spread out over several weeks. But be forewarned: hot weather greatly accelerates ripening, and the cherries can disappear before you know it.

But with the stem or without? The best I can say is that it really depends on how and when you plan to use them. For immediate consumption or pies, the fast and easy way (without stems) will do. If you plan to refrigerate your cherries for more than a day or two, then pick with the stems. It's slower but doesn't break the skin, so they stay fresh longer. Happy Picking!

SPRING FROST: THE GRIM REAPER

Fruit growers here in New Jersey dread freezing temperatures at bloom time. Spring frosts can kill buds or blossoms and devastate a crop. It happens on cold, still nights when ground-hugging cold air moves into the fields. If the night is clear and windless, fruit buds lose heat quickly, becoming colder than the surrounding air. The result is frost, which can occur even when air temperatures are above freezing.

Farmers have been trying to control frost since ancient times, when grape growers burned brush in their vineyards. Today's farmers sometimes use fans to mix lower-level cold air with the warmer air above. And sometimes they rely on irrigation, which is what I'm trying this year on my strawberries.

Irrigation is one of the most effective ways to keep frost at bay. As water freezes, it liberates heat. Farmers start irrigating when the air temperature is still above freezing. When the air temperature drops below 33 degrees, ice begins to form, and some of the heat liberated is taken up by the plants, keeping them a degree or so above freezing.

This process gives off considerable heat. A gallon of fuel burned in a heater releases 144,000 BTUs. That same gallon used in a diesel-powered pump can spray 14,000 gallons of water on a field. If all that water froze into ice it would release more than 16,000,000 BTUs — a 110-fold increase.

I'm enjoying the challenge of planning and constructing an irrigation system for protecting my strawberries. I'll need a water supply and reliable pump, but my new well and pumping system will be adequate for the job. Then there's the layout of sprinklers and piping in the strawberry patch. Fortunately, I have a wealth of printed information to guide me — my frost protection folder is now four inches thick!

It's important knowing when to activate the system: too early can result in over-irrigating, which is expensive and can damage the plants, while too late can waste the whole effort. I've consulted with some of my fellow farmers about this. Some get very little sleep during strawberry bloom time. They put a sleeping bag in their pickup truck, park out by the field, and wake up every half hour or so to check the temperature. There's no room for error: in extreme cases, temperatures can drop as much as nine degrees in as little as 15 minutes.

The trouble with this approach is that I like my sleep. The prospect of staying awake night after night, followed by working all day, has little appeal. Fortunately, I have a device that warns me if the temperature falls in my greenhouse. It dials my phone and announces, "The temperature is low." I have a spare device I'll use for the strawberries. When I hear the message, it means I'd better get out there and start irrigating.

This spring, if you drive by early some morning and see the irrigation running on the strawberries, you'll know why. And when you come back in May to pick strawberries, you'll know that, just maybe, those berries came from buds that two months before were safely under ice.

2004

STARTING OUT WITH A BANG

This year started out with a bang in January, when Pam and I bought another farm. The Johnson farm on Van Kirk Road is 65 acres of preserved farmland. We're delighted to add more land to our farming business, now called Mount Farms, the name of the farm my family owned in West Windsor before selling it in 1961. I've spent the spring clearing the overgrown hedgerows, putting up a deer fence (a major job indeed), and walking the farm to get the feel of the place. The fields had been farmed for years in corn, soybeans, and hay, so we're working hard conditioning the soil to eventually plant orchards and perhaps a wine-grape vineyard. That will be fun!

A major challenge has been finding water for such grand plans. We've drilled two wells that have come up dry. We're confident there's water there somewhere, we just have to find it. We'll be renting out the farmhouse for a few years, until a family member might want to move in. The farm is beautiful and offers many opportunities for enhancing our business. It's important to rotate vegetable crops between fields, so we'll benefit from the additional flexibility.

Early this year our daughter Tannwen and Jim Washburn became engaged. How great is that! Tanni and Jim have been friends since they were classmates at Lawrenceville School. Tanni returned from living in San Francisco for five years, and their romance blossomed. In August we had a wonderful engagement dance party for family and friends.

January also marked Pam's swearing-in ceremony for her second term on the Lawrence Township Council. This year Pam is serving as deputy mayor. It's been a great challenge and a rewarding experience to serve the citizens of Lawrence Township. There are plenty of projects to work on, and Pam has had the privilege of working with so many talented and dedicated residents.

Our banner year continued in May with the birth of Maya Mount Hanewald , the child of our daughter Reuwai and her husband, Mike. Maya is growing beautifully and has enthralled all of us. She and her parents spent much of the summer here on the farm — what a treat!

Topping off the year, our son, Mark, serving in the Army in Germany, was recently promoted to sergeant. He's been in the service for two and a half years, and we're very proud of his accomplishments.

The year isn't over — our fall crops are almost ready to pick, so there's lots of excitement yet to come.

WINTER WORK

At Terhune Orchards, the trees and bushes have shed their leaves in preparation for another season of dormancy, followed (I hope) by a glorious springtime of blossoms and pollination. As they settle in for a winter's nap, I'm headed in the other direction. Winter farm work, while less time-sensitive and hectic than work we do in the growing and harvest seasons, is at least as interesting and rewarding.

Every winter, without fail, we prune each and every tree, bush, and cane on the farm. Pruning, the selective cutting of a fruit plant's limbs or branches, is how a farmer directs the growth of his fruit crops. In the growing season we water, fertilize, and spray, but by then the biggest influence on the crop — temperature, rain, wind, and sun: in a word, weather — is beyond our control.

At Terhune Orchards, we have thousands of trees: 20,000-plus apple, 2,000-plus peach, 100-plus pear, 1,000-plus cherry, as well as 3,000-plus blueberry bushes and 10 acres of raspberries and blackberries. All pruning is done by hand. That's a lot of winter work.

There are as many opinions about pruning as there are farmers. Every winter I go to three or four professional meetings where pruning is on the agenda and on people's minds. The discussions can get "interesting" because every farmer, researcher, and extension agent is sure he's right.

Attending all these meetings means I can't do all the pruning at Terhune by myself. When I come home, it's my job to distill what I've learned, add it to what I think I already know, and come up with usable directions for the men who do the bulk of our pruning.

Apples are the most interesting trees to prune. A pruner must decide what type of branch to cut, where on the branch to cut, and how many branches to cut. All these factors affect the size, color, sweetness, and shape of a tree's apples. Tree size, the number of apples per tree, the number of apples per acre, how soon a planting comes into production, and a tree's productive lifetime are all directly related to pruning.

Prune a tree too much and it will be slow to bear; its apples will be large but lacking in color and sweetness. A minimally pruned tree produces smaller apples that also lack color and sweetness; its apples are prone to disease and insect damage, and the tree itself is weaker and may break under a heavy crop.

Which is to say, benign neglect isn't in an apple tree's best interest. For example, the big trees in the farm's parking area suffered from lack of attention this year. They ended up with a heavy crop of small apples, and with many broken limbs.

Pruning peach trees is comparatively simple. A peach tree bears fruit on one-year-old wood, so we leave as many healthy, vigorous, one-year-old shoots (pencil thin and 30 inches long) as we can.

Pruning pear trees is even less labor intensive. Pear trees are prone to fire blight, a disease that attacks young, succulent branches. (The branches look like they've been singed by fire, hence the name.) Fire blight can strike a tree dead in a very short time. Since pruning promotes vigorous new growth, the only solution is to prune hardly at all — just basic shaping and minor thinning. Otherwise, we leave the tree alone. Hopefully the fire blight will, too.

I'm a bit new at growing blueberries, but pruning basics are simple: if you want big, sweet, flavorful berries, the older canes are removed in rotation. If you want a lot of smaller berries, the older canes are left in rotation much longer. Customers prefer large berries and are willing to pay more for them, but the volume of large berries from a given harvest is much smaller, so the farm makes less money selling them. In other words, a small crop results in large berries sold at a higher price but generating less income, while a large crop results in small berries sold at a lower price but generating more income. What a dilemma! Each year I say to myself, "Let someone else decide how to prune these blueberries!"

Lots of variables affect a fruit crop. Since many of these variables (especially weather) are beyond a farmer's control, there's no sense worrying about them. In winter, at a certain point there's nothing more to do. Once we've finished pruning, I take satisfaction knowing we did everything possible to produce a crop that hopefully will please both us and our customers. Happy growing!

APPLE GROWING, ITALIAN STYLE

As I write this, Pam and I are flying home from a weeklong trip to study apple growing in the Südtirol, or South Tyrol area, of Italy. This Italian province is adjacent to the Austrian border and was part of Austria before World War I. Most people there speak German as their everyday language, and street signs are in both German and Italian. The most interesting aspect of the Südtirol, at least for me, is that its 7,000 apple growers are among the world's most skilled and advanced.

The centerpiece of the trip was the four-day conference of the International Dwarf Fruit Tree Association (I.D.F.T.A.). We divided our time between lectures and orchard tours. Here at home I get nervous enough when anyone knowledgeable about apple growing visits Terhune Orchards. Imagine what it must be like to have 200 of the world's top growers, researchers, and nurserymen visit from 18 U.S. states, 25 countries, and five Canadian provinces! Italian farming practices were on display for all of us to see: planting, tree training and pruning, spraying, harvesting, and marketing.

All of the orchards visited as well as our home base of Bolzano were surrounded by the snow-covered Italian Alps. The lower elevations and valley floors were covered with apple orchards. The hillsides were carpeted with grape vineyards, no matter how steep the slope. One afternoon I hiked up from town on what our guide listed as a "promenade." Huff, puff — more like a trail for mountain goats! I came across several people working in the vineyards but could not even begin to understand how farm operations like spraying, mowing, and harvesting are accomplished on such steep slopes. Maybe Italian tractors have better brakes (and drivers) than American ones.

One of the most interesting orchards we visited was covered in hail nets recently installed by the owner. He told us how, in four of the last eight years, hailstorms had pummeled the orchard, reducing the value of his apples from 30 cents to 6 cents a pound. The netting and wire/cable support cost $12,000 per acre, but he felt it was worth the expense.

Our group was hosted by the Tyrolean Fruit Growers. The I.D.F.T.A.'s annual conference is an unparalleled opportunity to expand one's knowledge of fruit growing and share it with others. I chair the association's research committee, which this year awarded grants totaling more than $40,000 for research related to dwarf apple and cherry rootstocks.

Our trip ended with hearty goodbyes to the many friends I've made in the I.D.F.T.A. over the last 27 years. I will be seeing them again next year — and doubtless learning more.

JOHNNY APPLESEED

I'm always a surprised by how many people think that apple growing is just a matter of planting a seed and then watching it develop. That was the way John Chapman (the real name of of the legendary nurseryman Johnny Appleseed, 1774-1845) did it, but things have changed since his day.

A tree grown from a seed taken from one of my best-selling apples won't produce the same apple. Almost always, its appearance (size, shape, and color) and taste will be different, and commercially speaking, inferior — fewer than one in a thousand would be worth cultivating. This is because apple trees don't stay true to type (fruit growers call this "true to name") from one generation to the next when they reproduce "the old-fashioned way," i.e., by honeybees carrying pollen from one tree to another.

Johnny Appleseed didn't care if his trees stayed true to name. But it's a primary concern of today's growers, who achieve uniformity by one of two horticultural methods, budding or grafting, which join either an emerging branch (bud) or top of the desired variety to a rootstock. Once the new, hybrid tree matures, it will produce apples identical to those of the parent stock.

Modern growers are also concerned about the size of their trees and the spacing between them. The oldest trees at Terhune Orchards, those in our parking area by the entrance, are more than 20 feet tall and planted 35 feet apart in rows 35 feet apart, which works out to 35 trees per acre. (Some of our older customers tell us this is what a "real" orchard should look like.)

A density of 35 trees per acre was standard until 40 years ago. Since then, growers have learned that smaller trees, planted closer together, will produce bigger crops sooner, and at lower cost. At Terhune Orchards, over the last 27 years I've planted apple trees at densities of 380, 670, 950, and even 1,675 trees per acre.

One big advantage of dwarf trees is that ladders aren't needed for pruning, thinning, and picking. Dwarf trees are much heavier producers than those old trees in the parking area because there's little wasted space between them. Best of all, they produce sooner. The old-style planting took 17 years to reach full crop, while today's smaller and more closely spaced trees can do so in as little as four years.

Closer plantings became possible with the development of dwarf rootstocks, which keep a tree small regardless of the variety budded or grafted. When I plant my trees two feet apart (1,675 per acre), I don't worry about overgrowing the space — the rootstock will keep them small.

And our friend Johnny Appleseed? Few of the seedlings he distributed to settlers in the Ohio Valley produced worthwhile eating apples, at least by today's standards. Yet settlers, most of them subsistence farmers, welcomed him anyway. That's because apples weren't grown for eating (unless cooked) but for making "hard" (alcoholic) cider. So the fact that his apples weren't edible scarcely mattered.

2005

APPLE PICKING

Many of us know the poem by Robert Frost, "After Apple Picking." This apple grower has a copy of it framed and hanging in his kitchen. But as much as apple growers look forward to the "after" part of apple picking, much work and planning goes into the "before."

This year at Terhune Orchards, we're blessed with a tremendous crop of apples. Now we have to pick them. Years ago, when Pam and I were just starting out, all apple picking was done using one-bushel wooden boxes. Each box held 40 pounds of apples. After pickers filled the boxes, an army of high school boys we hired leveled them off — for some reason this is called "cutting them down" — and stacked them on a wagon for transport to the farm's cold storage. The boxes were pushed along a roller conveyor into a large room refrigerated to 32 degrees. They were then stacked by hand, box by box, right to the 14-foot ceiling, leaving only enough space for the cold air to circulate.

It wasn't long before we changed over to bulk bins, handled by forklifts, with each bin holding 18 bushels and weighing 800 pounds when full. Which leads me to a question I've asked myself every year at harvest time: Will I have enough boxes (or in this case, bins) to collect and store our apples? This year, they're so many that I'm just not sure.

A related question: Who will pick all these apples?

The answer is simpler for me than it was for my father. His farm, where I grew up, produced only one crop, apples, which had to be picked over a six-week period. His pickers were hired for the occasion and came from all over, many from long distances, and he had to provide them with housing.

By contrast, Pam and I grow more than 30 different crops, and harvest time is spread over many months. And because we're a retail farm market with customers 12 months of the year, work on the farm continues all year. So when it comes to picking apples, our year-round employees are already in place.

My next question is more technical: When to pick?

I wish the answer were as simple as walking up to a tree, grabbing an apple, and crunching down on it to determine peak ripeness. But it's not. The time to pick an apple is mainly determined by the consumer. Pick-your-own customers want apples ready to eat, right then. The crunch test works fine for pick-your-own sales.

Picking apples for sale later on, in the Farm Store, is another matter. Picked too early, an apple is immature and has yet to develop its best flavor. Picked too late, it won't store worth a darn. Apples mature slowly up to a certain point — then the ripening advances rapidly and can't be reversed. The trick is to pick and refrigerate apples at full maturity, but just before the start of rapid ripening.

There are multiple ways to determine an optimal harvest date. One method is pretty straightforward: I count the number of days since the tree bloomed. Every apple variety has an average number of days between bloom and peak ripening; that average varies little from one year to the next, whether the growing season has been hot or cold, wet or dry. (One indicator I *don't* rely on is color, which weather conditions can greatly affect.)

Other methods are more technical — as Pam says, I'm a sucker for technology. I use one handheld device to measure the firmness of an apple's flesh. I use another to measure the concentration of sugar in its juice. I also have a device to measure an apple's ripening rate, which determines its suitability for storage based on the concentration of ethylene gas in the air gap around the seeds. (I withdraw an air sample with a needle inserted into the apple.)

Another measure of an apple's ripeness is its ratio of starch to sugar, which continually changes as ripening progresses. I cut an apple in half and spray the insides with an iodine solution. After a

TERHUNE ORCHARDS GALLERY

Pam and Gary, daughters Reuwai and Tannwen, and son Mark, ca. 1980. Reuwai and Tannwen are now business partners with their parents, and Mark is completing a 20-year Army career that included three combat tours in Afghanistan.

Pam and Gary, 2005, with daughters Reuwai and Tannwen, their husbands Mike Hanewald and Jim Washburn, and granddaughter Maya.

Pam and Gary with a bushel of their signature crop, ca. 2006.

Pam and Gary, ca. 1985.

Showing off Granny Smith apples, 2011. Back row: Jim, Maya, Reuwai and Tess, Mike and Sasha. Front row: Tannwen and Becket, Pam and Gary.

Gary pruning grape vines.

2016, from left, top row: Jim and Tannwen with twins Clay and Haddie;
Gary and Pam; Reuwai and Mike. Bottom row: Maya, Tess, Shasha, and Becket.

Pam and Gary, ca. 1990.

Gary planting strawberries, a late-summer ritual.

Jennifer and Fiona Swope in the picking garden.

The Apple Barn, 2017: Ruewai, Maya, Mike, and twins Tess and Sasha; Pam, Gay, and Becket; Tannwen and Jim and twins Haddie and Clay.

Eirene Merritt-Valaris with goat and guinea fowl.

Pam in front of the Farm Store.

2021, from left, Tess, Mike, Reuwai, Sasha, Maya, Pam, and Gary;
Tannwen, Jim, and Beckett with twins Clay and Haddie.

Pick-your-own strawberries.

Terhune dogs on Farm Store porch.

Gary and Pam on their 50th wedding anniversary, June 2017.

minute or two, the starch turns dark while the sugar stays light. Comparing the results to a photo-maturity chart tells me what I need to know.

Like many growers, I use a combination of all of the above — from the crunch test to the latest cutting-edge technology — to determine when to pick.

Despite all our preparation and effort, as an apple harvest progresses it can take on a mind of its own. Workers come and go, rain keeps us from picking, our retail farm market takes every available hand, and the carefully planned harvest sequence falls behind schedule. Then it's a matter of working as hard as we can — and hoping for the best.

THINNING APPLES

Each year in May, something happens at Terhune Orchards that makes me cringe. It's time to thin apples. I hate doing it; I get stressed and grouchy (or so says my family) — in short, thinning makes me a nervous wreck. But I have to do it. Otherwise, we'd be left with small apples at harvest, possibly broken-down trees, and, worst of all, the likelihood of a very light crop the following year.

Thinning apples is the process of removing some of the small apples from a tree early enough in the summer so the remaining apples can grow to a larger and more marketable size. Mother Nature provides a fruit tree with many more flower buds than it actually needs. A medium-size apple tree might be able to support and bring to maturity about 700 apples. But the tree may have 1,000 to 2,000 flower buds, with each bud capable of producing five flowers and thus five apples. That's a lot of apples. Most years, spring frosts and other environmental factors take their toll, so not all of the flowers become apples. It's a good thing there are so many buds; some survive — enough to make a good crop. Often, though, many more apples survive than a tree can support. That's when thinning becomes necessary.

Growing up on an apple farm in West Windsor, I did a lot of thinning. In those days, all thinning was done by hand. My father was pleased to have four sons — eight extra hands in the orchard — to thin apples, which was what my brothers and I spent much of our summer "vacation" doing.

After moving into a summer house my parents bought at the Jersey Shore, we commuted to the farm daily to thin apples. Thinning involved positioning and repositioning a heavy, 22-foot ladder as we worked our way around a tree, then moving the ladder from one tree to the next. We scrambled up and down the ladder, picking and picking over the course of a long, exhausting day. The work was also mentally demanding: How many apples to thin off and how many to leave? Decisions, decisions! Bone tired, all my brothers and I wanted to do on the ride back to the Shore was sleep, but our father's maniacal driving kept us wide-eyed awake. It's impossible to say how many times my family's entire male line came close to obliteration.

Apple trees tend to bear a lot of apples one year and few apples the next. Thinning breaks this alternate-bearing cycle. At the same time a tree is growing apples for this year, it's developing buds for the following year. As an apple grows, its seeds exude a hormone that moves up the stem and into the wood of the tree. Depending on how much hormone the wood absorbs, buds will evolve into either leaves or flowers. More apples mean more seeds and higher hormone levels, which stimulate more buds to evolve into leaves. Thinning makes for fewer apples, which mean fewer seeds and lower hormone levels, so more buds evolve into flowers on next year's tree; once pollinated, the flowers develop into apples — many more than the tree would have produced without the previous year's thinning.

Thinning in most orchards is now done with a combination of hand thinning and spraying. Sprays take advantage of a tree's natural tendency to drop some of its fruit in June. It mimics the natural process and stimulates the tree to drop more fruit. We follow up with thinning by hand.

Spray thinning is not an exact science, however. It's greatly affected by weather before and after application. Spraying can work marginally, just right, or too well. If marginally, we do more hand-thinning to compensate. If just right, we do less hand-thinning, or none at all. If *too* well, it means we've over-thinned; there's nothing we can do to compensate, and the result will be fewer apples than we'd like.

I try to remain positive at thinning time and stay cool around my family. Thinning *usually* works as it should. It's just another part of what I regard as the world's best job — growing apples.

ZIP, SLAM, BAM!

A recent apple growers' trip to Washington State included a stop at an apple packinghouse, where I watched in fascination as a huge machine assembled cardboard apple boxes — zip, slam, bam. It took me back 50 years. This one machine completely accomplished my boyhood job of making boxes on my father's farm — only about 50 times faster.

For a long time, growers in Washington and Oregon have sent their fruit to be stored and packed at large warehouses. Eastern growers, like my father, packed their own apples. During the frantic harvest season, little packing was done while the fruit was picked, transported, and stored in refrigerated rooms. When harvest ended, packing began. It continued all winter and often into spring, sometimes ending as late as May.

My father's cold storage and packinghouse was on Route 1 in West Windsor. The storage rooms could hold 175,000 bushels of apples, and the packinghouse was filled with packing machinery from the Wayland Company of Winchester, W.Va. This equipment washed, dried, sorted, and sized the apples. All the packing was done by hand.

My father built a second-story addition to the packinghouse for storage. This was also where I assembled the cardboard boxes. My after-school and Saturday job was "making boxes." The boxes arrived at the farm flat and in bundles from the manufacturer, Union Bag and Box Company. I would open the flattened boxes and staple the bottom flaps together. I then threw them down a large hole in the packinghouse ceiling.

Once the space below was filled, I made as many boxes as I could ahead of time, for the next day. I was 13 years old but rated myself the fastest box maker on the farm. My output increased dramatically after my father bought a motorized stapling machine and a monorail conveyor system to transport the assembled boxes down to the packing crew.

Cardboard boxes were a departure from the wooden boxes previously used for storing and shipping apples. The transition occurred about the time of my 13th birthday, so I had experience with both. Apples packed in wooden boxes were individually wrapped in ten-inch squares of oiled purple paper. Wrapping apples was an art, and doing it rapidly was difficult. I got pretty good at it, but never as good as our best workers. And nobody did it better than Dollie Mae Jackson — her skills were highly valued. Dollie's husband, Ivory (Ira) Jackson, was another valued employee, and in later years I often worked with him in the orchard.

Wooden apple boxes came in two types — "western" (7/8 bushel) and "eastern" (1 bushel). Apples in westerns were individually wrapped. Those in easterns were packed loose. Wooden boxes on our farm were either purchased used and then refurbished or assembled new from parts purchased from a box manufacturer. In either case, a specialist named Gid Davis did this work on our farm. Gid spent most of the year in Florida and traveled to New Jersey once a year to work for my father. He sometimes drove a truck on the farm, but mostly he was our box man. His hands were lightning fast. He was very skilled at sanding the sides of the used boxes to make them appear new, and he had a 1952 Mercury. To my 12-year-old eyes, a '52 Merc was just about the ultimate in cool. I don't remember ever wanting a particular car more. Gid kept it immaculately clean and polished and parked it near his work site so he could listen to the radio while assembling boxes. I could never understand why that didn't drain the battery, but his '52 Merc always cranked.

One special item Gid used was a nail stripper. Buying nails in bulk means the nails come in a jumbled pile. Picking up one nail results in getting your fingers poked by the points of other nails.

A slow and painful process! Somehow the nail stripper shakes the nails down so they hang in strips for easy (and painless) access. Neat! It was another thing my 12-year-old brain had trouble grasping. I saw a nail stripper in a museum during my recent trip to Washington State. It brought back lots of memories.

After the apples were washed, dried, sorted, sized, wrapped, and boxed, it was time to prepare the boxes for shipping. Lids were nailed closed, and boxes for overseas export were strapped at each end with wire, then labeled and stenciled.

Labeling evokes a lore all its own. Before 1960, every packinghouse had its own colorful and descriptive label. Many apple growers today collect old labels — some have hundreds. I think the "Mount Farms" label was one of the best. The labels, 8 by 11 inches, were applied to the ends of the boxes using a paste of flour and water. Labeling was one of the jobs waiting for me when I got home from grade school.

We stacked the day's output of packed boxes in long rows in front of the packinghouse. After labeling and stenciling, they were loaded onto a truck for delivery to a pier in New York City. Getting the label on straight and marking the product with the name of our family farm was deeply satisfying. It ranked close to the top of my favorite jobs on the farm — right up there with stenciling.

Boxes containing apples for export had to be stenciled. A shipment's code number was punched into an oak-tag sheet to create a stencil. The number was then stenciled with black ink onto the side of the box. At first, my father ordered stencils pre-punched, but later he bought his own stencil-cutting machine.

I don't remember my father as a patient person, but he must have been. I often had something to talk to him about just as he was finishing a stencil. A moment's distraction, a wrong letter punched, and he would have to discard the stencil and start a new one. I also tried his patience one day when we had two different lots of apple boxes for shipping, each lot requiring its own stencil. I liked stenciling and was quick at the job, and when I got to the end of the first lot I went on to the second before anyone could tell me to stop and change stencils. Oops!

A stencil also included the name of the ship receiving the apples. Seeing those names in the packinghouse was unbearably romantic to a 12-year-old compulsive reader of books. Even now, I wonder how I kept from stowing away in the back of a truck headed for the piers. But I was needed on the farm.

2006

Re-covering the Greenhouse

In late fall, the outdoor world at Terhune Orchards changes dramatically. Our fruit trees and bushes are dormant now and have shed their leaves; our vegetables and flowers have all been picked or killed by frost. Everything has gone from green to brown. But the daily miracle of growth doesn't cease, it just moves indoors. And so my thoughts turn to the greenhouse.

Terhune's greenhouse isn't that big. Just three years ago, we doubled its size to 5,000 square feet, but as greenhouses go, that's still small. However, it's a very active place. Starting in September and October, we plant hundreds of freesia bulbs. These gorgeous ornamentals grow slowly all fall and winter at 55 degrees. They bloom in January and February. Their blooms, all in a row on the stem, are the most amazing colors! It's a real winter pick-me-up.

Sometime this fall, after the frantic apple harvest and pumpkin season but before it gets too cold, we need to re-cover the greenhouse. We use a double layer of poly, stretched over the greenhouse frame and fastened at the edges. The existing plastic has been on for three years — about the limit. Ultraviolet radiation from the sun turns the plastic cloudy, reducing the amount of sunlight that can pass through. UV also weakens the poly and makes it more likely to tear in a windstorm. In winter, this would mean the end of the freesias.

The trick to re-covering is doing it on a calm day, warm enough so the plants inside don't suffer, and then working like heck Whatever we take off we have to replace by the end of the day. Cold temperatures at night would ruin everything inside.

Our greenhouse is two bays wide. Each bay is covered by two sheets of poly 28 by 100 feet. Each double layer is fastened securely around the edges and then attached to a fan that blows air into the space between the layers. This creates a taut air pillow that keeps the plastic from flapping in the wind and provides insulation as well.

Hopefully, if the re-covery goes well, we can start on our next crop. Freesia, cyclamen, and later some spring bulbs will be growing in the greenhouse all winter, but there's still space for lettuce.

We started growing lettuce last winter — red leaf, green leaf, Boston, romaine. Fifty-five degrees turns out to be just right for lettuce as well as freesia. We plant one crop after another, seeding and re-seeding all winter long. Each crop takes 8 to 12 weeks. We then pick it, sell it, and start in again. Even though it's indoors, an actively growing crop keeps me happy until spring, when life outside begins anew.

Storing Apples

Many fruit and vegetable crops are extremely perishable. Farmers must pick and then sell them in a short period of time. Take leaf lettuce. We've been growing some great leaf lettuce this year — everyone loves it. But if it's not sold within a day or two of harvest, it's destined for compost. Refrigeration extends its shelf life, but only slightly. The same is true for many of our other crops, apples excepted. The ability to store apples for many months with no loss of flavor or quality puts them in an entirely different category. Partly because of their year-round availability, apples are among the nation's most valuable fruit crops.

In colonial times, before refrigeration and before farmers knew how to control for disease and insects, apples didn't keep very long. Some went bad on the tree before they were picked. But most apples grown back then weren't destined for eating. They were made into cider, which at the time meant alcoholic cider. Effectively, apples were "stored" in a liquid state. Most farmers had a few apple trees, and if a farmer couldn't make cider himself, he took his apples to a neighbor who could and brought it home in a barrel. Once the cider fermented, the alcohol acted as a preservative; the minimum alcohol content to do the job was about 8 percent.

Hard cider was the nation's favorite beverage until the late 1800s, when beer eclipsed it.

Although apples were mainly grown for cider, they were also eaten and used in cooking. A farmer stored his apples in a root cellar, often built into the slope of a hill. The constant, cool temperature and high humidity maintained the apples until winter. A root cellar also kept apples from freezing, which accelerates spoilage.

Early in my farming days at Terhune Orchards, I got to know an older apple grower named Ralph Del Santi. Ralph, who farmed in Morris County, told me of his "storage method." Ralph had a large spreading tree near his farm buildings. In the fall he stacked his baskets of apples under the tree and that was it. He did this mostly with varieties that were harvested late in the fall, when the weather turned cool. The tree protected the apples from direct sun and sheltered them from frost, both of which would spoil the apples. Ralph told me his apples "kept pretty good." I wasn't totally convinced, but it took Ralph just a month or so to sell all his apples, so it worked for him.

Mechanical refrigeration was a big advance in apple storage. With our home refrigerators, freezers, and air conditioning, mechanical refrigeration is something we take for granted, but when it came along in the early-to-mid 20th century it was a welcome innovation for apple growers. It allowed them to control temperatures for different apple varieties. Red Delicious and Stayman store best at 30-31 degrees, for example, while McIntosh stores better at 33 degrees.

The size of a refrigeration unit matters: bigger is better. Apples keep best when cooled to their ideal temperature within 24 hours after picking; smaller units take longer to cool apples and may condense too much moisture from the surrounding air, causing shrinkage.

The latest advance in keeping apples is "controlled atmosphere" storage. Oxidation hastens ripening, and C.A. storage sharply reduces oxygen levels in the surrounding air, significantly increasing storage time. Early C.A. units stored apples at 5 percent oxygen levels (compared to 20 percent in the air we breathe). The latest technology reduces oxygen levels to 1 or 2 percent, enabling apples to keep up to a year or more. I've heard that experimental units at the Cornell College of Agriculture have stored apples successfully for four years. That sounds impressive, although I'm not sure what "successfully" means.

Readers who know me can see where I'm heading. It's like my relationship with tractors — I can never have enough of them. The fact is, we need new cold storage at Terhune; our present unit is now too small for all the apples we harvest, and I truck many of them to a friend's cold storage in southern New Jersey. I've dreamed of building new cold storage for several years. During a trip to Nova Scotia last winter, I visited two farms with just the type I want. Next year, customers may well see new construction here: state-of-the-art cold storage.

HAYGROVE HIGH TUNNELS: CONTROL OF NATURE

One of the most "interesting" aspects of farming is its relationship to weather. Of course, farmers depend on good weather for the success of their crops, but severe weather can take its toll on them. Heat waves, cold spells, too much or too little rain, high winds — bad things happen, and when they do there isn't always much a farmer can do about it.

On cold spring nights we can protect our strawberries from frost by spraying them with water from our irrigation system. At Terhune Orchards we also have our weatherproof, 5,000-square-foot greenhouse for growing winter flowers and produce.

This spring we're installing a new type of enclosure to protect one of our most popular crops. It's going up now, and while not quite finished I'm already getting questions about it. "What are you building out there? It seems to be near the cherries." The answer is, yes, it is near the cherries. In fact, it's *over* the cherries. It's called a Haygrove high tunnel. I purchased it from the Haygrove Company of Herefordshire, England, and its purpose is to protect our cherries from my friend and nemesis, the weather.

Many of our pick-your-own customers have seen the devastating effect weather can have on cherries. When they're ripening in the final two weeks before harvest, cherries undergo a growth spurt. Their cells expand so rapidly that the skin is stretched to the breaking point. If we get a significant amount of rain, water saturates the cherries so they swell even more, and the skin cracks, exposing the flesh to decay — making for an unappealing mess. Three years ago, we had three days of rain before cherry harvest and 100 percent of the cherries cracked. Not one was picked! Just awful, a total loss.

Enter the Haygrove tunnels. Right now they're halfway through construction and just rows of high metal hoops over the cherry trees. In a week or two we'll cover the hoops with clear plastic secured by an arrangement of crisscrossed ropes. The covers can be raised or lowered as conditions demand. In times of high temperature or strong winds, for example, we can vent the tunnels by pushing up the plastic, opening space at ground level.

Since we started work on the tunnels, I've realized they can also protect our cherry blossoms from killing spring frosts.
(Something we want to avoid: no blossoms, no cherries.)

The tunnels could also advance our harvest date: we could cover the trees early, raising the average temperature under the tunnels. Steve Blizzard, a fruit-growing friend in California's Central Valley, did this recently. Steve's orchard is huge — hundreds of acres versus our two acres — and his crop is packed and sold wholesale, with most of the cherries exported to Asian or Pacific Rim countries. It's a tough market, and harvesting his cherries a week or two ahead of the competition gives him a significant advantage.

That said, I'm thinking that harvesting our cherries early might not be the best idea. We start pick-your-own strawberries right before cherry time, and if the two overlapped, things could get hectic.

2007

BLUEBERRY BLUE

Right up front I should tell you that our granddaughter Maya loves the color blue. From her earliest days, it's been blue for her all the way.

This predilection for blue just might have come from her grand-father's passion for growing blueberries. At Terhune Orchards we have two acres of blueberries. That might not seem like much but believe me, it's a lot of blueberries — millions! They're about the most satisfying crop I grow.

Growing blueberries is intriguing. They actually are not sup-posed to grow well in our part of the state. They grow wild in the Pine Barrens, where they were first domesticated, and thrive in that region's soil, which is highly acidic, rich in organic matter, well drained, and with a high water table, in some places just two feet below the surface. Our soil has none of these characteristics.

Planting blueberries begins with a two-year-old plant pur-chased from a nursery. I bought my plants from Michigan. Two acres spaced at 3 by 10 feet gives us room for 3,000 plants — an entire tractor-trailer load.

Blueberries require acidic soil. Their roots can't absorb nutri-ents from soil with PH levels higher than 5. Pine Barrens soils have levels between 4.5 and 5; the soil at Terhune Orchards measures 6 to 6.5. We lower the PH by adding sulfur. Because soil rebounds to its natural state, we add sulfur every year.

We also have to compensate for our soil's relative lack of organic matter, which in Pine Barrens soils runs between 7 and 9 percent or higher; our upland soils are about 2 percent. You may have noticed the mountain of wood chips here on the farm — we apply those chips around our blueberry plants every year.

Water management is important, too. Blueberries don't like "wet feet," so we ridge up every row 8 to 12 inches so heavy rainfall runs off quickly. We also have to deal with drought — during the growing season, our water table can sink 14 feet below the surface. No blueberry roots go down this far, so we've installed a trickle-irrigation system; it provides the roots with water in just the right amounts to keep them happy. We irrigate as needed, often daily.

Growing blueberries requires patience. It takes a blueberry plant five to seven years to produce a good crop. Experts say to remove a plant's flowers the first year to encourage growth. I followed that advice, but doing so killed me.

Birds love blueberries — they flock to them and can wipe out a crop in just a couple of days, so at harvest time we enclose our entire two acres of plants with plastic netting. It's an expensive and time-consuming operation, but it makes me happy seeing the birds flapping around outside the net, making a fuss about being excluded.

When at last it's time to pick, about the third week in June, the first berries are amazing. They are huge and exceptionally tasty — tart as well as sweet. There aren't very many, only a few per bush. Our veteran pick-your-own customers make sure to arrive early for the limited supply.

Most fruits need picking within a week after they've fully ripened, but blueberries can stay on the bush for a month or more over an extended ripening season. Some of our customers come weekly over the summer, picking from the same bushes as the berries ripen.

Granddaughter Maya will be moving here from Baltimore this summer, just in time to pick and eat blueberries, the fruit of her favorite color.

ONE HUNDRED FORTY YEARS OLD

I recently attended a 140th birthday party. Although my friends tell me I don't look that old, my passion for farming links me to the founding, on January 19, 1867, of the Princeton Agricultural Association, which I currently serve as president. The birthday party, held at Drumthwacket, the governor's residence, was a meeting of the association commemorating its 140th anniversary.

It was nice having the meeting at Drumthwacket because the association's organizational meeting took place there, too. That first meeting was hosted by Charles Smith Olden (1799-1876), a former governor of New Jersey who owned Drunthwacket at the time. It was also nice having my wife, Pam, and our daughter Tannwen and her husband, Jim, in attendance.

The agenda included a talk by one of our members on topics discussed in the association's early days as recorded in meeting minutes, some of which can be found in Princeton University's

Firestone Library. The first meeting addressed the "Proper application of manure to land," noting that wood ash increases yields threefold ("good") and that hair, presumably from farm animals, makes "excellent" manure; farmers should avoid tan bark ("no good") as well as water-soaked leaves and "strong hen manure."

Minutes of the February 1912 meeting drew my attention, observing in passing that "Mr. Mount, a very successful apple grower, was present and gave a very interesting talk." This Mr. Mount was my grandfather, William Mount. I knew my father had been a member of the association but had no idea about my grandfather's connection.

We followed our meeting with a tour of Drumthwacket and a dinner at Windrows, a retirement community near Forrestal Village where one of our honorary members, Ed Van Zandt, is a resident. It was good to see Ed — we miss him at our monthly dinner meetings.

The Princeton Agricultural Association carries on today much as it has for the past 140 years (although we no longer travel to meetings by horse and buggy). We have 24 members, roughly half of whom are active farmers. There are no dues, although every two years a member is responsible for hosting (paying for) the dinner and recruiting a speaker. We have two officers, a president and secretary-treasurer. Presidents come and go, but secretaries have real staying power — we've had just five in the association's entire existence. Our current secretary, Charlie Grayson, has been at the job for close to 20 years, and his predecessor, Duncan Campbell, held the position for 65 years. Duncan, a farmer from Belle Mead, was a fine gentleman who died several years ago, at the age of 106.

Charlie, our after-dinner speaker, gave an interesting and informative account of farm life in the early 20th century as detailed in his historical monograph, *Gleanings from the Past: Memories of an Old Farmer*, available from the Van Harlington Historical Society, of Montgomery Township.

Membership in the Princeton Agricultural Association connects me with farmers past and the important (if sometimes underappreciated) role they've played in our community. It connects me, too, with my father, who, due to his untimely death just two months after I graduated from college, I never got to know in my adult years.

And as I learned at the association's last meeting, it also connects me with my grandfather.

STRAWBERRY TIME

Strawberry harvest season is just around the corner. Strawberries are one our first crops each year and also one of our best. Red, juicy, sweet, refreshing — all those adjectives apply to strawberries.

When days warm and strawberry plants emerge from winter dormancy and begin to grow, the crop's success depends on work we did the previous year. It begins in June, when we decide where to plant next year's crop. So that pick-your-own customers won't have to walk too far, we choose a field close to the Farm Store (where they pay for what they've picked). We avoid planting in a field where strawberries were grown in the last few years. Planting the same crop in the same place year after year allows diseases and insects to build in the soil, while also depleting essential nutrients.

Next, we plow the site, make raised beds in the soil, bury trickle-irrigation tubes in the beds, and cover the beds with black plastic. Raised beds elevate the plant roots, protecting them from flooding during heavy spring downpours. The black plastic prevents weeds from growing and keeps berries off the soil, a source of disease. Together, the raised beds and black plastic help the soil warm quickly in spring, promoting vigorous growth. The trickle-irrigation tubes dispense water and nutrients throughout the growing season.

Now we're ready for the strawberry plants. The first plants go into the ground in late July. These plants have exposed roots and are purchased from a nursery; they were dug up the previous fall and kept in cold storage (33 degrees) at the nursery until shipped to us. In late August we do a second planting, this time with strawberry plants growing in containers; they were started at the nursery in June and are shipped to us in flats.

We care for the plants throughout the summer and fall — watering; controlling for weeds, insects, and disease; and keeping out rabbits, deer, and Canada geese (which view strawberry plants as candy).

In late October, we cover the plants with "floating row cover," a white sheeting to protect them from severe winter temperatures.

In spring, we watch for the first strawberry flowers to appear under the row covers. When they do, we remove the covers so bees (which we import for the occasion) can pollinate the flowers.

The crop is at its most vulnerable in early spring. Strawberries bloom early, and a hard frost can kill the blossoms — no blossoms, no berries. So as soon as we remove the covers we install an overhead watering system. It's counterintuitive, but spraying water on plants on a cold night keeps them from freezing. As long as water is continuously applied and the air temperature doesn't get too, too cold, the plants will stay above 32 degrees. Trust me, it works.

After four or five weeks the strawberries are ready to pick.

It's important that, while growing, strawberries get the nutrients required for optimal size, color, firmness, and taste. This winter I attended a lecture by Steve Bogash, a Penn State agricultural extension agent whose specialty is strawberry production. Steve advises growers to analyze their strawberry tissue weekly throughout the spring to know what the plants are absorbing (or not) from the soil. If particular nutrients are lacking or insufficient, they can be added to the water supplied by the trickle-irrigation tubes. I'll probably be doing some tissue analysis this spring.

All this to grow strawberries. It's complicated, painstaking, and expensive. But, if we do it right and the weather cooperates, what a reward. Come on out and pick some strawberries this year. They should be ready mid-May.

2008

FARMLAND PRESERVATION

The Mounts are celebrating the permanent preservation of our 26-acre pick-your-own orchard on Van Kirk Road this winter. This means that all four of the properties we farm on Cold Soil and Van Kirk roads are now permanently preserved.

The importance of this to my family can hardly be overstated. To plan for the future and maintain a viable enterprise, farmers need stability, especially those like us who grow perennial crops such as apples, peaches, pears, cherries, and berries.

New Jersey's farmland preservation program began with legislation and a bond referendum in 1981. The program provides incentives to farmers to continue farming their land instead of selling it to developers of residential and commercial properties. Under its terms, farmers can sell their development rights to the state if they agree to a deed restriction precluding them or future owners from using the property for purposes other than agriculture. Here in Mercer County, the first farmer to take advantage of the program was Ed Hendrickson, whose former dairy farm is now a thriving nursery.

The program benefits the state and community in many ways. Crops grown on New Jersey's preserved farms don't have to be trucked in from out of state because they're grown right here. A preserved farm doesn't require additional municipal services such as education for the families who might have lived there had it become a housing tract. And farmers can use the payments received for development rights to invest in operations, helping assure success going forward. We'll be using our payment for new construction — namely, a bigger barn and cold storage for apples, a longtime dream.

To date, the program has paid farmers roughly $1 billion for property rights and has preserved more than 1,700 farms, totaling almost 179,000 acres. New Jersey has become a leader in the nation's efforts to preserve farmland.

For Pam and me personally, our decision to participate in the program makes it far easier for future generations of Mounts to farm the land. We're lucky to have children who are interested in doing so. It remains to be seen if they'll continue in the family tradition, but the opportunity is there if they choose that path. Happy Holidays!

WEEDS, GLORIOUS WEEDS

Whether you're a homeowner planting ornamentals or a farmer planting a crop, chances are you wind up with the same complaint: If only my plants could grow as well as the weeds! At

Terhune Orchards, the time is approaching to begin my annual battle against weeds.

Weeds are devilish. They rob my crops of space, sunlight, nutrients, and water, provide refuge for damaging insects, and look terrible. Not to mention the poison ivy that makes me itch, and Canada thistle — *ouch!*

When I first became a farmer, it was common practice to "clean-cultivate" a peach orchard. I did this by going back and forth with a tractor hauling a heavy disc, up and down and across the rows, until all the weeds were uprooted and buried. Discing loosened the soil down to six inches, eliminating weeds and the competition for water and nutrients. What I didn't realize at the time, however, was that peach trees are shallow-rooted: many of their feeder roots (the smaller ones that take up water and nutrients, as opposed to the larger anchor roots) are just three inches below the surface. As I drove back and forth with the tractor and disc, I was chopping off these essential roots. The result was sickly trees and smaller peaches.

Then there was rain. In my first year of farming, I didn't fully appreciate the importance of rain and how too much of it can negatively impact crops. I never thought it could rain seven inches in one week, as it did that first July, right during peach harvest. And it kept on raining all summer. I watched a lot of my topsoil wash away. It can take nature a hundred years or more to create one inch of topsoil. Distressing.

Then there was "lugging," a term you've probably never heard. We resort to lugging if peaches are picked after rain has inundated a clean-cultivated orchard. The soggy ground makes it impossible to drive a truck into the orchard; instead, we park the truck at the edge of the orchard and carry ("lug") the peaches to it as they're picked. Picking becomes a team effort: one picker, one lugger. The picker's job is to pick and the lugger's job is to slog through the mud with a full basket of peaches to the truck. Even 33 years later, I can still hear the pickers calling whenever they filled a basket: "Lugger!"

Fortunately, we've evolved better ways to deal with weeds. We plant a thick-growing sod between the rows — one that we can drive and walk on easily. Under the trees, we spray a herbicide that keeps weeds from sprouting. The herbicide remains active during the two or three months when most weeds sprout, then breaks down chemically. With no weeds to rob the trees of water and nutrition, we're able to reduce irrigation and fertilizer.

Eliminating weeds is also an effective way to control insect pests. One particularly damaging insect takes a small bite out of a peach when it's smaller than a pea and just starting to develop. As the peach grows, the area around the bite doesn't. The fruit becomes distorted and misshapen — we call the unsightly result "cat-facing." It used to take spraying an insecticide to prevent this injury. Peach growers, however, have discovered that during its growth cycle, the cat-facing bug spends part of its life on the tree and part of it on the ground, specifically on broadleaf weeds — sort of a city house/country house thing. By using a weed spray under the tree and tight, vigorous grass sod between the rows, we've eliminated broadleaf weeds in the orchard, breaking the cat-facing bug's growth cycle.

Weeds remain a problem in our attempts to grow vegetables organically. The U.S. Department of Agriculture won't certify produce as organic if the farmer uses chemicals to combat weeds or insects. We recently began organic production of vegetables on eight acres, and I'm still learning what it will take to defeat weeds without resorting to chemical herbicides. Hopefully, I'll be clever and energetic enough to prevail.

I have dreams of someday growing some of our apples organically. I tried it twice before — starting in 1978 for three years, and in 1984 for four years. Both times I was unable to produce appealing apples at reasonable cost. One of my biggest problems was weed control. At some point I'm going to try again — I have some new techniques and materials to work with. Stay tuned.

2009

THE NEW BARN

Today was a red-letter day. This morning I went to pick up the building permit to begin construction on our new barn. This project has been under consideration for the last 20 or 30 years, and finally we're starting.

My brothers tell me I often make things more complicated than they need to be. I don't necessarily agree, but then, this barn really is turning out to be more complicated than anticipated. A significant portion of its interior space will be devoted to storing apples in temperature-controlled rooms for sale later in the fall or even well into the following year. For many years, we've trucked our apples to Mullica Hill, in Gloucester County, for cold storage on the farm of my friend Carl Heilig. Carl, the co-owner with his father of Heilig Orchards, mainly grows peaches, a summer crop sold soon after picking, so come early fall he has excess space in his storage rooms.

It's a good deal for us, and we're grateful to the Heilig family for helping us all these years. There are problems with this long-distance relationship, however. The time between picking apples here and placing them in cold storage at Heilig Orchards can be three or four days, and every day delayed reduces their storage life by one or two weeks. And the long, two-way drive on county roads — bump, bump, bump — risks bruising the apples.

We're also dependent on John Hart of Rosedale Mills to truck the apples back and forth. We thank John for this vital service, although it can't be convenient for him to drop what he's doing to help us out, sometimes on short notice.

The long and short of it: We'll be far better off having our own cold storage at Terhune Orchards.

Apples are best stored in a system that controls for temperature (ideally 32 degrees), humidity, and oxygen levels. You need a lot of refrigeration capacity to get the apples to 32 degrees fast after they've been placed in storage — about twice what it takes to actually maintain them at that temperature once they've reached it. The system has to monitor and control humidity so the apples don't lose moisture, causing them to shrivel. Finally, the system needs to keep oxygen levels at 2 percent, which slows further ripening to a crawl. (The air we breath is 20 percent oxygen. Ripening, the conversion of an apple's starch to sugar, is a function of oxidation.)

All of the above features are contained in a technology called controlled-atmosphere storage. That's what we'll have in the new barn. It will allow us to keep apples as firm and crisp as the day they were picked, all the way to the next harvest season.

THE NEW BARN II

It's been a busy and exciting fall at the farm, with a lot of attention focused on our new barn. Customers love it, frequently commenting, "They don't make barns like this anymore." They bombard us with questions such as *Who designed it?* (Jerry Ford of Ford3 Architects, Princeton), *Who built it?* (Sylvan Stoltzfus Builders, of Lancaster, Pa.), and *What's the exterior siding?* (cypress).

The roof is standing seam-painted steel. The dry-storage area's interior is timber framing, same as our 160-year-old barn. The wooden beams are hemlock, with oak pegs holding it all together.

The timber-frame section is for storing "stuff," otherwise known as Gary's Treasures. (These are various farming-related items I've collected over the years and have no intention of discarding — who knows when I might need them?) We'll also be storing items currently housed in the old barn, since we're working on plans for that to become our new winery. There's been some family discussion as to the sole use of the timber-framed area for storage of Gary's Treasures. It's turned out to be a wonderful area for events — dinners, barn dances, parties. Gary's Treasures may wind up in the back, packed tightly together.

The section of barn on the left as you face it holds three cold-storage rooms. Two large rooms keep fruit at 32 degrees; one smaller room can keep melons, potatoes, tomatoes, and peppers at 55 degrees, or apples at 32 degrees, or frozen items at zero degrees. Two 30-horsepower compressors power this magnificent assemblage of coldness. The storage rooms' walls and ceilings are six-inch urethane foam to keep heat infiltration at a minimum.

One of the storage rooms maintains the atmosphere at 2 percent oxygen to keep apples fresh over an extended period. (See my previous column for details.) We keep it locked and make sure the air is restored to normal 20 percent oxygen before anyone goes into it to remove apples (to prevent them from fainting, or worse). The room has to be air tight to maintain its low oxygen level. We monitor air-tight integrity by increasing the air pressure inside the room, then squirting soapy water on the exterior wall to see if any bubbles form. A few have; we're working on the problem.

Cold storage right here on the farm is turning out even better than anticipated. Unlike previously, when we stored apples at Heilig Orchards in South Jersey, we can now place them in storage the evening of the same day we pick them. And when we're ready to sell them, we just open the door and there they are.

We have two things still to do on the barn. First, we'll be installing solar panels on the south side of the roof to generate electricity to offset the cost of running the refrigeration equipment. Second, we'll install lightning rods. My friend Dick Lee, of Lee Turkey Farm, in East Windsor, visited last week to see the new barn. He reminded me that many a barn has been lost to fire caused by lightning. Lightning rods reduce the chance of lightning striking the building, and if it does, they provide a safer path for the lightning to reach ground.

RAMBLING WITH FARMER GARY

Pam and I used to listen religiously to "Rambling with Gambling," a New York–based morning radio program — Do any of my readers recall it? The show's weatherman would proclaim a certain day to be one of the ten best of the year. He did this often — maybe 20 or 30 times a year!

Today was one of *my* ten best days on the farm this year. I hosted a tour for sixth-grade students of the peach orchard across from us on Cold Soil Road. The orchard is part of a 100-acre property owned by the gas company Williams Transco, which a few years ago purchased the land (a former farm) to build a compressor station for boosting pressure in its pipelines. The station itself takes up 20 acres. Williams Transco has set aside the remaining 80 acres for conservation (protecting wildlife habitat and the Stony Brook corridor) and agriculture (our peach orchard).

Every year, Williams Transco, along with D&R Greenway and the Lawrence Conservation Foundation (the nonprofits overseeing the conservation work), and Terhune Orchards invite local fifth or sixth graders to tour the property. The students explore Stony Brook (getting muddy and wet) and the compressor station, then spend time with me in the orchard as my "assistant peach growers."

These kids are joyfully uninhibited — full of ideas and eager to ask questions. I introduce them to Integrated Pest Management. As its name suggests, I.P.M. is a multifaceted, systematic approach for dealing with crop-damaging pests. We've used it for years on our peaches as well as other crops. I start with my standard corny joke, asking, "What's worse than a worm in your peach? Answer: "Half a worm." The students respond to this with words like "Yuk!" and "Gross!," but they get the joke, and laugh. When I recently spoke to adults about I.P.M. at the Whole Earth Center in Princeton, I told the same joke, but no one laughed — they didn't get it.

The worm (or half-worm) in the peach is no match for I.P.M. The worms hatch from eggs laid by female moths after they mate with males. We talk about how males find females — it's not by accident, I remind them — and end up comparing the female scent, or pheromone, with teenagers' perfume and how both attract males. Every year without fail — and with just a nudge from me — the students come up with a way farmers can use this information to prevent male moths from homing in on females.

The answer: place a pheromone dispenser in every tree, thereby overloading the orchard with female scent. When the male moths show up, the scent overwhelms them. They become hopelessly confused and cannot find the females. The result: no mating, no eggs, no worms, no need to spray.

Peach farmers have other nifty I.P.M. strategies for dealing with insects which allow us to minimize or even eliminate the use of pesticides in our orchards. They enable us to grow peaches with less water and fertilizer (by killing competing weeds under the trees) and to keep mice from damaging tree trunks without poisons (again, by killing weeds — mice avoid bare ground, which exposes them to predators.)

We use I.P.M. on most of our fruits and vegetables. And every year, my visiting "assistants" figure out on their own how it works.

2010

LET THE SUN SHINE

I think of Terhune Orchards as a "solar farm" in the sense that, through photosynthesis, it converts sunlight to carbohydrates (the fruits and vegetables we grow).

This year we're using sunlight in a different way. Last fall we finished installing the solar electrical system (think of it as a "solar garden") on the roof of our new barn. We situated the barn so that one roof faced directly south for maximum solar benefit.

As soon as work began on the barn, we contracted with a company to install the solar system. But how big did we want to make it? Because the barn was new, we couldn't gauge our needs from past records of electrical use. We had no experience with the cold-storage rooms planned for the barn, so estimating how much power they'd need was a shot in the dark (no pun intended). Their usage on a year-to-year basis will largely depend on how many apples, peaches, pears, and other produce we store in them, and for how long.

We knew that the credit received from the power company for generating our own electricity would drop once we started gener-ating more electricity than we used, so we were wary of building too big — more solar panels, more expense. After thinking it over, we determined we'd probably need all the electricity we could generate, so we filled the roof with panels.

This week the power company connected our system to the grid and we started generating electricity. A meter measures elec-tricity in and out. Meanwhile, the solar panels sit there on the roof, doing their thing. Not much goes on at night, but on a sunny day, oh boy!

Today we installed a monitoring screen in the Farm Store to show what's happening on the barn roof. On your next visit you can see for yourself — so long as the sun is shining.

From the Grapevine to You

This fall, Terhune Orchards unveils its latest project — making and selling our own wine in the old barn at the home farm on Cold Soil Road. We plan to open our wine store in September.

Farmers in the state have been able to make and sell wine since the passage of the New Jersey Farm Winery Act of 1981. The law permits farmers to make wine from any kind of fruit they grow (grapes, apples, peaches, or whatever) and sell it on their property.

The original legislation also allowed farmers to sell their wines at up to three other locations. One of the first farm wineries in our area was LaFollette Vineyard and Winery, in Belle Mead. Established in 1986, it was owned and operated by John and Mimi Summerskill. Terhune Orchards was one of LaFollette's three other sales outlets, and John and Mimi became our good friends. They were an amazing couple, both gone now, with a vision far beyond the ordinary. Mimi was an educator, author, and political activist as well as an exceptional cook: a meal at the Summerskills' was an unforgettable experience.

Our venture into the wine business began in April 2006, when we planted a vineyard — 4.5 acres of wine grapes — on our new farm on Van Kirk Road. We purchased this 65-acre property seven years ago, in 2003, from Dave and Libby Johnson. (The Johnsons owned the property for 50 years, and not surprisingly, neighbors still call it "the Johnson Farm." They probably will for a while.) The property has greatly increased our farming potential. In addition to the wine grapes initially planted there, 40 percent of it is now devoted to organic production — mostly vegetables, but as of this year including two acres of organic apples.

I love farming and the challenge of growing a new crop. We now grow some 36 different crops, having added roughly one a year, on average, since starting our business 35 years ago.

Every crop is different, and each has its own set of challenges. The first step for growing grapes (or any crop) is testing the soil for nutrients and the percentage of organic matter, which greatly affects a crop's ability to absorb nutrients. A soil test also reveals the presence or absence of nematodes. These tiny, wormlike insects are bad news in two ways: they compete with the plants for nutrients, and can severely weaken or kill them by transmitting harmful viruses. Fortunately, the Van Kirk property was free of nematodes.

My next challenge was finding water for irrigation. Once established, grapes vines don't need much water, but for the first couple of years they're vulnerable to drought; without irrigation, a dry summer like last year's could have wiped out our fledgling vineyard.

Wanting to find water and actually finding it are two different things. I am, without question, very good at *not* finding water. My first two drilling attempts came up dry. Unfortunately, the cost of drilling is the same whether you find water or not. On our third attempt we found a spot that produced 14 gallons per minute — not a lot, but enough for the young vines. Pam says I should quit while I'm ahead and forego more attempts to drill wells for a while. She may have a point.

CASTING CALLS AT TERHUNE ORCHARDS

Our life here at Terhune Orchards has its amusing moments, especially when the photo/video/commercial production people come calling.

Whenever a company asks to use our farm for some commercial purpose, Pam invariably says yes; this isn't the response it would likely get from me. She said yes, for example, when Guinness World Records asked us to host a photo-shoot of the world's fastest pumpkin carver (record time: 24.03 seconds) doing his thing on one of our big pumpkins. Actually, more than one pumpkin — the shoot lasted three and a half hours (to be exact, 3 hours, 33 minutes, and 49 seconds), and during that time the guy went through 50. At roughly 40 pounds each, that's literally a ton of pumpkins. Carving all those pumpkins included cleaning them out; when he was finished, it was our job to clean up the huge mess of pumpkin innards. For such a special occasion, I suppose, it's not surprising that the photographer and his two assistants were imported from England. (Then again, Guinness is a British firm.)

Another company that got to Pam first was Fox TV, which wanted to film an episode of its reality series "Kitchen Nightmares" here and at Hannah & Mason's, a restaurant in Cranbury. The idea was to serve everything fresh — "Jersey Fresh" — in February. Maybe because they're New Yorkers, the show's producers seemed to think that food grows in supermarkets. Providing them with fresh produce in the middle of winter was a challenge, but we were one of the few farm markets open, so they spent a day shooting at the Farm Store. When they also asked us (that is, Pam) to set up a farmer's market in front of Hannah & Mason's, we of course obliged. The market looked great and attracted a lot of attention, and the next thing we knew, people were dropping in to shop. Unfortunately, we lacked a permit so couldn't sell any of the produce on display.

At the end of the episode, the show's celebrity chef, Gordon Ramsay, gave us a nice plug when he bit into one of our apples and said to the camera, "That's a *really* good apple."

Our biggest casting call occurred when a film company shot a TV commercial over three days in mid-September, maybe our busiest time of year. It was a huge operation, involving 200 people, only two of whom actually worked for the company — actually, they *were* the company. Everyone else was freelance, or as we say in the farming game, "day haul." The crew had a person for every job as well as a backup person. Even the woman who combed the actors' hair between takes had a backup.

Two large trucks arrived and unloaded enough equipment to fill our driveway and parking area. The crew spent an entire day shooting in the Farm Store while our customers were sent around to the back of the store to shop. They spent another day shooting a scene in the kitchen/dining area of the farmhouse, where Pam and I live. The space got a major, if temporary, makeover; most of the items were removed and replaced with other items so it conformed to their idea of what a "real" farm kitchen should look like. This included replacing our kitchen chairs with a collection of mismatched ones.

Once shooting started, we learned that the most of important of the 200 people was the cameraman — like 95 percent of an army supporting the 5 percent who do the fighting. We also learned the value of backups. On the final day, the cameraman got sick (he actually wound up in the hospital), but his backup came into his own and finished the job.

The company paid us for using the farm, although the fee was surely a fraction of what it cost in lost sales. We had three days with some very nice people, however, and our eyes were opened to a whole new world.

We never did get to see our farm in a national ad campaign. The product advertised, an anti-inflammatory drug called Vioxx, was pulled from the market shortly after the commercial was filmed.

2011

GOING BUGGY

"A bug is a bug is a bug." You can say the same thing about crop disease, although it doesn't roll as well off the tongue. As a farmer growing fruits and vegetables in central New Jersey, I pay a lot of attention to harmful bugs and diseases. We live close to eastern ports, where many of them enter the country, and we have a moist, humid climate that allows them to thrive.

This is my 37th year as a farmer, and every year I face the same problems, along with some new ones. I'm sometimes asked why bugs are such a problem. After all, humans have been growing fruits and vegetables for thousands of years. It's true that in our country's first 100 years or so, most people lived and worked on farms. (Today it's something like 2 percent.) Crops were primarily grown to feed the farmer's family, and cosmetic standards were low to nonexistent. Not many fruits and vegetables were eaten raw, and bad spots were simply cut out before cooking. Apples and pears were mostly consumed in a liquid state, as hard cider or perry (cider made from pears).

But farmers today grow crops to sell; their produce has to please a customer's eye, and the damage and disfigurement caused by pests and diseases can seriously impact a farmer's livelihood. (Last year a customer told me she throws out any ear of corn with a worm in the tip. It never occurred to her, apparently, to cut off the tip, throw it out with the worm, and cook the rest.)

In the middle of the last century, farmers began using pesticides, which by reducing insects and diseases led to bigger and better crops. But pesticides weren't panaceas. Some of them lasted too long, without breaking down chemically. Some caused harm to animals and humans and killed the good (predacious) bugs along with the bad.

My father farmed over five decades, from the 1920s to the '60s. Thinking back on it, I'm amazed at how little he knew about insects, disease, and pesticides. If something worked, farmers used it, often unaware of any negative side effects.

Today's farmers have far more access to far better information from state cooperative-extension agencies — and New Jersey's, under the aegis of the Rutgers School of Agriculture, is one of the best. As noted before, Rutgers extension agents have been my mentors in the application of Integrated Pest Management (I.P.M.), a wholistic approach that minimizes the use of pesticides. One I.P.M. technique uses pheromones, sexual attractants (perfumes) emitted by female moths, to lure males. A synthetic pheromone inside a sticky trap attracts male moths, whose presence in turn tells us the brief window of time when the moths are active. My dad knew that codling moths (adult apple worms) were generally active in June, so from late May through early July he sprayed weekly. My pheromone traps tell me exactly when the moths are active, and I spray just once.

We also use pheromones to disrupt mating. To use a football analogy, think of it as "flooding the zone." During mating season we attach packets of pheromones on trees throughout the orchard. The pheromones attract male moths in great numbers, but with so much of the scent wafting about, it's impossible for them to zero in on the females. End result: no mating, no eggs, no worms, no more spraying for codling moths.

Bug problems never end. One of my recent concerns is the brown marmorated stink bug. An invasive species from Southeast Asia, it appeared in the U.S. eight years ago and has spread to almost every state. Stink bugs are devastating to fruits and vegetables — they are highly mobile and omnivorous and can easily go from one crop to another. They have few natural predators and high resistance to pesticides. Last year, stink bugs moved into our orchards right at the end of harvest, three or four days before the last apples were picked. On our later varieties we had 55-percent damage from stink bugs. I'm hoping that Rutgers can find a creative way to deal with them.

"LEARNING" A CROP

At Terhune Orchards we grow 36 crops sold in our Farm Store, at farmer's markets, and to schools and restaurants. Learning about crops has kept me engaged in my work for 36 years and counting.

When Pam and I started out in 1975, we made friends with Bob and Dottie Dobbs, farmers in Camden County. They were older than us and had been farming for many years. Bob grew 15 or 20 different crops. At the time, I was growing just three — apples, peaches, and pears — and couldn't understand how he managed. How could he keep all those crops separate in his head and know what to do for each, and when to do it?

In the early 1980s, Pam and I realized we had to grow more crops. To make our business prosper, we needed a greater variety of produce to sell. There was a gasoline shortage at the time, and for customers to burn two gallons of gas to drive here for one gallon of cider didn't make sense. We've been adding crops ever since — one or two a year, our most recent being wine grapes. Every crop is uniquely challenging, and for every new one there's a learning curve. My favorite author, John McPhee, wrote in one of his books about riverboat captains learning a river one turn at a time. That's how I think of learning a crop.

Although I grew up on a farm and am the 10th generation of my family to farm in this area, knowledge of farming isn't innate. My father grew only one crop, apples. I helped him in the orchard and with other apple-related chores. I learned how to work but can't really say I learned how to grow apples. I knew what I was doing but not the *why* of what I was doing.

My most important teacher has been the Rutgers Cooperative Extension system. Every county in the country has an agricultural extension office. In New Jersey it's connected to Rutgers, the state's land grant university. Established by federal legislation in 1914, cooperative extension has provided assistance to farmers (and now homeowners) ever since. Its contributions to American agricultural productivity cannot be overstated, and for me it's been personal. When Pam and I started out, we were lucky to have an agent in Mercer County who specialized in fruit production. He visited our farm once a week, on average, for the first few years. Having someone like that "in my corner" was so helpful.

In addition, I started going to meetings and building my farming library. The New Jersey State Horticultural Society has sponsored an annual convention for many years, and for the past 36 years it has joined with the Pennsylvania and Maryland societies to sponsor a regional annual meeting in Hershey, Pa. I go to every session I can and have hardly missed a year. I'm also a regular at meetings of the International Fruit Tree Association, which I've attended 35 years in a row; this year, an older member told me how well he remembered Pam and me, years ago, in the front row, bombarding the speaker with questions. Closer to home, I attend informal "twilight meetings" of fruit and vegetable growers at different farms in our area.

I've also been blessed with talented and dedicated employees who have taught me so much. One, Emiliano Martinez, has been a mentor in the art and science of growing a wide range of vegetables. I have learned to listen.

I mentioned my farming library. Books about growing wine grapes, our latest crop, are like grapes in a bunch — too many to count. I have a good number of them. My farm workers laugh when I tell them to wait a minute while I run to my office to look something up.

Growing so many crops spreads me a bit thin. I'm not as good at growing all of our crops as I'd like. But I wouldn't have it any other way. Growing just one or two crops — I couldn't do it. This week I finished my master plan for the vegetables we'll be planting this year. Except for annuals like asparagus and rhubarb, they're all in the plan, which includes a line item for every variety and a detailed schedule for planting and replanting (some are planted eight times in a season). The total number of entries is now north of 650. Next year I hope to add artichokes to the mix, so the number will grow.

SMOOTHING THE LAND

My latest farming adventure isn't planting, growing, picking, storing, processing, or selling a crop. It's getting ready to plant a crop.

Last year I planted 4.5 acres of wine grapes on a section of our new 65-acre farm on Van Kirk Road. I wanted to expand the planting to an adjacent field but ran into a problem. The field has a gentle slope, so it's well drained except for a low spot where water collects after heavy rains, creating "Lake Terhune." The lake, 6 to 12 inches deep, is temporary and usually dries up after a week or so. Still, there's no way grape vines will tolerate sitting there that long with their feet in the water.

I didn't know what to do about Lake Terhune until I talked to my friends at the Natural Resource Conservation Service, a federal agency that, among other things, helps farmers solve land-use problems. They suggested "land smoothing." The plan they helped me develop has three phases. First, 8 to 12 inches of topsoil is pushed to the side. Then the subsoil is graded to eliminate Lake Terhune while still providing a gentle slope. Finally, the topsoil is pushed back in place. The project in its entirety covers ten acres. That's nothing compared to a big real-estate development, but for us it's like the pyramids.

We hired a contractor, Tom Posch of Patriot Excavating, in Farmingdale, and set to work. Tom's people arrived a few weeks ago and started moving dirt. The project has been progressing nicely. Then, this week, we had nine inches of rain! All work stopped, and we're now waiting for the land to dry.

There's a good side to the delay. My three-year-old grandson, Becket, lives next to the ten-acre field. He loves any sort of heavy equipment and thrills to the sight of Tom's bulldozers pushing soil back and forth. Like his grandfather, he enjoys watching them smooth the land.

2012

SPUDS

When my brothers and I were growing up on a farm in West Windsor, we didn't think of ourselves as "farmers" but as "fruit growers." (Our father grew only one crop, apples.) This distinction between "growers" and "farmers" remains prevalent to this day, at least in the minds of fruit growers.

My father had many friends who grew potatoes in our area, but they were "farmers," not growers. Every year he invited his farmer friends to come over on Thanksgiving morning and hunt on our place, which covered 350 acres between Route 1 and the Delaware-Raritan Canal. My brother Lee and I looked forward to their arrival and were allowed to join in the hunt with our bows and arrows, which we made from apple tree shoots, called suckers. The pheasants and rabbits were quite safe from us, but we loved tagging along. Following the hunt, my mother served a hearty breakfast to everyone — 15 to 20 hungry men, plus me and my brother. We did better on the breakfast than we did hunting.

Times change. I don't hunt anymore, and I've become "a farmer." I grow lots of different kinds of fruit — apples, peaches, pears, cherries, blueberries, raspberries — but included in our 36 crops at Terhune Orchards are many vegetables, including potatoes. I've been growing potatoes for the last four years. One of many things I like about them is their wide range of sizes, shapes, and colors. They come large, small, and extra small; round and oblong; white, red, blue, rose, and yellow (skin); and white, blue, yellow, and purple (flesh). Each variety has its own subtly distinctive taste. It's an interesting crop.

I was over-enthusiastic this year and planted 18 different varieties. I also planted a lot of each variety — to the point where, now that it's time for picking my beloved apples, many of our apple bins are filled with potatoes. So much for the fruit grower/farmer dichotomy.

Pam encourages me to curb my enthusiasm next year: "We don't have room in the Farm Store for all those potatoes!" But we're enjoying them for dinner — the different appearances, textures, and flavors are a treat to this fruit grower/farmer's eyes and taste buds.

The first seed catalogs for next year's planting are now arriving in the mail. They include several new potato varieties I want to try.

FRIEND AND MENTOR: VERNON HORN

Vernon Horn died this winter at the age of 79. He was my mentor in many things and was generous with his ideas, enthusiasm, and friendship. His influence has guided me in much of what we've done here at the farm.

I first met Vernon when Pam and I lived in Bucks County, near Doylestown, after returning to the States from Micronesia, where we'd spent most of the previous three years as Peace Corps volunteers. I was now working as a real estate salesman. One day I came home from work to find Vernon in our kitchen arguing with Pam about education. The debate was passionate — so much so that they barely said hello. The initial reason for Vernon's visit had nothing to do with education, however. He owned a quarry in sight of the house we were renting and had stopped by to complain that his crews weren't getting much done because of a major distraction: a certain young woman (Pam) mowing the lawn in a bikini.

That first debate was not the last with Vernon, as we soon became friends with him, his wife, Edith, and their four children. We visited the Horns for Sunday dinners during the five years we lived in Bucks County; for several years after our purchase of Terhune Orchards and move to Lawrence Township, we continued meeting for dinner at our place or theirs.

Vernon's enthusiasm for life was stunning. His ideas were, as we say today, "outside the box." I haven't known anyone so self-directed as Vernon — like his decision to buy an old farm property and turn it into a stone quarry.

I had taken a job I disliked and was becoming a "do the minimum" sort of guy. I worked for my brother Bill, the most generous boss anyone could ever have, but brokering real estate deals — making my living by taking a percentage of what a seller was paid for his property — just wasn't for me. Vernon's outlook toward his work was so different. Every Sunday at our dinners, he restlessly fidgeted, anticipating the work week that started the next morning. He loved his work and the equipment that went with quarrying and contracting.

Once, when Pam and I planned a vacation trip to Key West but lacked the money to fly, we decided to drive. Vernon and Edith (he called her "Chicken") asked if they could drive down with us, with the idea of flying back once we arrived. Pam and I welcomed their company and help with the driving and gas. We didn't realize it meant driving nonstop all the way to Jacksonville, where Vernon insisted on stopping so he could look for quarrying equipment for sale. Somehow, he knew the name and location of every dealer in town. We visited them all while Vernon gave us a running commentary about every truck, bulldozer, loader, and rock crusher.

His attitude rubbed off on me. Buying a farm and becoming a farmer was an "outside the box" thing to do in 1975. As a graduate of Princeton, I had the idea that I ought to be a doctor or lawyer or captain of industry. Vernon helped me see that I could be a farmer, and that thinking it worthwhile was reason enough to go ahead.

When Pam and I purchased Terhune Orchards, we knew apple cider would be a big part of our business. I had never made cider and had never seen it made, but I knew enough to see that the cider equipment that came with the farm needed upgrading. Vernon came over to help. We worked all day, all night, and all the next day building a new cider plant.

Pam and I had no money to purchase the farm but somehow managed to borrow what we needed. Some of the financing came from the Farmers Home Administration's farm ownership loan program. Members of the local F.H.A. committee paid us a visit and looked over the property. They knew how tough it was to farm in our area — how farmers were selling out to developers because they couldn't make a profit — but they believed in our potential and approved the loan. Going so deeply into debt was daunting, but Vernon's tongue-in-cheek comment put our concerns in perspective: "I never wanted to be a millionaire, I just wanted to *owe* a million."

Vernon is gone now, but his enthusiasm for life and willingness to help us is something Pam and I will never forget.

WATER, WATER III

Back in 2001, I wrote several columns about my efforts to find water for irrigating our crops. Since then, I've expanded our irrigation system, drilling more wells and burying miles of plastic pipe to keep the water flowing when we need it.

My interest in water supply goes way back. I grew up on a farm in West Windsor that bordered the Delaware and Raritan Canal, which now supplies water for about a third of New Jersey's residents. When Pam and I were in the Peace Corps in the late 1960s, one of the projects I worked on was a water supply system for the small island in Micronesia where we were stationed. (I'm pleased to report that now, 45 years later, it's not only still working, but the islanders have doubled its size.) In the 1980s, I was a New Jersey water commissioner with responsibility for the D&R Canal I knew so well from my childhood.

Water availability for agriculture is a huge issue, not just for me but for the state, the country, and the world. In comparison with the rest of the world, we have a lot of water in the U.S., and New Jersey has a better supply than most states. But not all of New Jersey — in some areas, including ours, water remains an issue. Over the years, most of my attempts to find water have been failures. We would locate a spot capable of supplying two to three gallons of water per minute — O.K. for a house, perhaps, but not nearly enough for a farm. I've been lucky to find one good site at our pick-your-own orchard on Van Kirk Road as well as a not-so-good, but adequate, site at our other farm on Van Kirk, where we grow wine grapes and organic vegetables. To find water, I've twice enlisted the help of dowsers, who used wires or forked branches held in their hands; also a hydrogeologist, who used maps of subsurface rock formations to advise us where to drill, and a geologist, who used specialized instruments to measure subsurface patterns of electrical interference.

Experiences like these have led me to several conclusions. First, no one really knows where to find water in our area. There are no aquifers below the surface — water is found only in fracture zones in otherwise solid rock. Second, if you do find water in sufficient quantities for farming, you should go out and buy a lottery ticket right away, because it's your lucky day! And finally, if your wife realizes how much you're spending on all those dry holes ($15,000-plus each), you're in for some serious discussions about how many more you can drill.

This summer is proving disastrously dry for many farms in the U.S., particularly in the Midwest. In New Jersey, conditions were very dry in June and the first half of July. Luckily for us, the work I had done drilling wells and burying distribution lines paid off — we had water available for our crops. However, it is still a lot of work to get everything watered. I also have to coordinate my use of water for the fruit and sweet corn with Emiliano Martinez, our longtime employee who grows most of our vegetables. Between us, we keep the water flowing day and night. It involves moving a lot of equipment, and we get pretty tired. When an inch of rain fell on July 20, it was a blessing. Farmers call that "a million-dollar rain."

I've worked with agents of the U.S. Natural Resource Conservation Service to develop our irrigation system. They've helped me be a better steward of our water resources while still providing sufficient water for our crops. One neat technique I've learned from them is soil-moisture monitoring. We've buried moisture sensors at 26 different spots. Usually we place two sensors next to each other, one shallow and one deep. Every day or so, one of our employees goes around with a meter to check the sensors, and we post the resulting readings on a chart. This helps me avoid under- or over-watering.

I no longer fear having to watch, as in 1998, some of my crops die for lack of water. I'm thinking of drilling one more well to provide a better supply of water to one of our farms. If we find any, I'm buying a lottery ticket.

THE QUEEN

At Terhune Orchards, when we talk about the Queen, many would think we're referring to Pam. That's not far wrong, but there's another Queen — the Queen of Fruits, the peach.

I have a love-hate relationship with peaches. I love their taste, their aroma, their texture, and their brief, intense season. But I hate with a passion how hard they are to grow and a peach tree's short lifespan. It's taken me a while to learn how to grow and care for peach trees. They are very susceptible to insects, root diseases, and low-temperature injury in the dead of winter. I've learned to mound up each row to keep the roots from getting saturated with water, and we actually paint the tree trunks white to keep them from warming and starting to flow sap on sunny winter days. If that happens, the trunks can split when the temperature drops at night. I don't have to work at making winters warmer — that's happening without my help, but the other problems have taken a while to address.

I grew up on an apple farm — apples were all we grew, 300 acres of them. My father and uncle once planted about 20 acres of peaches but quickly decided peaches weren't for them. My uncle had a summer house in the Poconos and our family had a house at the shore. Apples are a crop they could leave on weekends in summer — my father and uncle liked that. Not so peaches. Peach harvest comes right in the middle of summer. Peaches need to be picked, sorted, packed, and marketed every day. So they tore out the peach trees, planted more apple trees, and life returned to normal.

When Pam and I bought the farm in 1975, it came with apples, pears, and peaches. It was good to have all three because cash flow was tight in the summer, even though growing peaches bound us 24/7 to the farm. In those days, three crops were all we had to worry about — nothing like the 36 crops we grow now.

We grew many types of peaches, including heirloom varieties like Blake, Sunhigh, Yellow Hale, White Hale, Raritan Rose, Summercrest, Iron Mountain, to name a few. Some were greenish, some were ugly, but they all tasted great. Summercrest was oblong, with a greenish cast — ugly, lumpy, but what a taste. Customers in the know kept it a secret — they were afraid the Summercrest would go too fast. Then there was Iron Mountain, a late variety that was ready to pick a month after all the other peaches were done. We only had a few trees, and the scarcity of Iron Mountain increased their desirability in our customers' eyes.

How well I remember our first fall at Terhune: Pam sitting on the floor of the Farm Store, eight months pregnant with Tannwen, our second child, and with our three-year-old daughter, Reuwai, sleeping in a playpen nearby. Customers were leaning over Pam, demanding a basket of scarce Iron Mountain peaches. Invariably, the first customer wanted three baskets, much to the dismay of Pam and the other customers.

The nature of our heirloom peach trees showed in their age and health. They were old, tall, weak, and poor producers. They were also short-lived, even for peach trees. Many were so tall that not a single peach could be picked without a stepladder. Because of this, our harvest crew consisted of pickers and luggers — the pickers doing the picking and the luggers lugging the baskets from the tree back to the harvest truck, a 1939 Chevrolet, with a 1.5-ton stake body — the same truck you see near the Farm Store every winter, filled with firewood for sale.

Since those early days, we've planted and replanted our peach trees many times. The new varieties live longer — 18 to 20 years instead of 12 — and through vigorous pruning we manage to keep them low enough so ladders aren't needed for harvesting. And we've expanded our offerings with donut peaches and nectarines (peaches without the fuzz).

We've learned a lot about caring for peaches and have greatly reduced our dependence on pesticides. We still need fungicides because peaches are susceptible to decay, but pesticides are almost out. We used to spray to control for peach moths, but now we use pheromones to keep males and females from mating.

Our trees are beginning to show their age, and in order to maintain a steady supply of peaches we will have to plant new trees soon; they'll take three or four years to come into production, and once they do we'll take the old trees out. I've been attending meetings on new varieties, talking to Rutgers specialists, and am ready to order trees.

Our peaches are no longer ugly or green — the old varieties are gone. The new varieties are more pleasing to the eye and at least as pleasing to the palate.

2013

Getting Ready

Springtime at the farm is a conundrum and a kerfuffle. I look forward to spring all winter and can hardly wait for its arrival. Then when it comes, POW! It's like an avalanche. There's so much to do — all at the same time — to prepare for the new growing season. It's all about getting ready.

One of the first tasks is plowing. I grew up on a fruit farm, and we didn't even own a plow. Any plowing occasionally needed — to put in a new orchard, for example — was done by an uncle who owned a plow for tilling the soil for his vegetable and field crops. Or the plowing was contracted out.

Before I'd done any plowing myself, I assumed it was easy. I now know better. I have learned, for example, that timing is critical. Plowing too early compacts our high clay-content soil, leaving large, hard clumps and a field unsuitable for planting. Conversely, if I plow too late, after the soil has dried out, the plow doesn't penetrate but just skids along the ground. I also plow to turn under weeds and soil-enriching cover crops, but I need to do this early. If I plow too late, the weeds and cover crop will grow too tall for the plow to fully bury them; they will keep on growing, competing with the vegetables for water and nutrients.

After plowing comes planting. We don't start planting vegetables until the danger of frost is past, so the first things I plant are fruit trees. There's nothing I like doing more. This year we planted a new peach orchard, a thousand trees totaling 20 different varieties. We caught a lucky break in the weather, when the soil wasn't too wet, and planted on March 31, all in a single day.

We did the job with a seedling planter pulled by a tractor. The planter, which resembles a miniature plow, cuts a furrow as the tractor pulls it along. The operation was a team effort from start to finish. Charlie drove the tractor while Emiliano sat on the planter, inserting the seedlings into the furrow. Scott, Alfredo, and Noe walked beside the planter, feeding Emiliano the seedlings and ensuring they were grouped together by variety and placed in proper sequence. Eric and Juan walked ahead, marking the rows with stakes so the rows would be straight and correctly spaced (a matter of pride for any farmer). Kevin, George, and Felipe walked behind, adjusting the seedlings' depth and straightness. My granddaughter Maya, meanwhile, ran up and down the rows, retrieving the stakes and returning them to the truck. A great day's work!

As spring advances, our attention turns to grapevines and vegetables. This year we planted 1,400 grapevines. It will be three or four years before they begin producing harvestable grapes. No machine planting for grapevines — the spacing must be exact. Again, Eric got all the rows lined up (he has an eye for this), and we planted the vines by hand.

We plant vegetables either by seed or as transplants started in the greenhouse. Often, we cover the transplants in "low tunnels" made of a fine-mesh fabric supported by metal hoops three feet high. The covers protect the plants from late frosts.

Frosts! A late frost can easily kill a newly planted crop or any crop in flower. Strawberries bedevil me in this regard. We put white, porous fabric covers over the berry fields in winter, but when the plants start to bloom, the covers have to come off so the flowers are exposed to bees and other insects for pollination — otherwise, no strawberries. Trouble is, the last frost usually occurs after we uncover the berries. We think of May 10 as our last frost date, but in recent years it sometimes comes early. Last year it was April 23, although this year it was May 14.

After uncovering the berries, we immediately set up a sprinkler system in the field along with a thermometer that triggers a device to call me if the temperature drops below 32 degrees. I then go out to the field and turn on the water. Ice may form on the strawberry plants, but as long as the water keeps coming their temperature stays above freezing, and they survive. Most years the system calls me two or three times — I can handle it. But this year it called 12 times, and always in the middle of the night, when I was sound asleep.

My spring to-do list includes a plan for controlling diseases, pests, and weeds. I evaluate potential problems in consultation with advisers from Rutgers Cooperative Extension. Workers need to be hired and materials ordered. Some of our crops are organic and some are conventional, but the problems are the same — the difference is in how we deal with them. This year, to control weeds in our organic vegetable plots, we'll be laying ground cover between rows. The ground cover is a woven black plastic that lets water through but prevents weeds from growing. It's kind of expensive but should last many years.

One proven pest-control method is "mating disruption." We use it in both our conventional and organic plots to control the larvae, also known as "borers" or "worms," of various moths, including the codling moth, oriental fruit moth, peach tree borer, lesser peach tree borer, leopard moth, and grape root borer moth. Traditional controls involve spraying with either conventional or organic pesticides to kill the worms. Mating disruption is far more clever. It takes advantage of the fact that male moths seeking females find them by following their scent, or pheromone, through the air. We put a synthetic pheromone dispenser — a small plastic tube — on every tree in the orchard. The male moths, when they arrive, are confused by the abundance of scent and can't find the females. No mating, no egg laying, no worms, no spraying. Great! Mating disruption actually works better than spraying. It costs a bit more, but I believe it's worth it.

Plowing, planting, planning. They all come at once. We get fantastically busy, but I wouldn't have it any other way.

Harry and Margaret

Harry and Margaret Schaafsma have been gone a while now, but we remember them fondly. They were among our first farmer friends after we bought Terhune Orchards 38 years ago. The Schaafmas lived near us on Cold Soil Road, in a farmhouse at the end of a driveway so long it put them in the neighboring township.

Harry had been a dairy farmer most of his life. He worked every day, milking his cows morning and evening. I once asked him if he and Margaret ever took time off. He said that once, in the 1950s, they spent a day at the beach. But of course, he had to milk his cows before they left, and again when they got back.

95

Harry and Margaret were wonderfully good-natured, and they encouraged our efforts as beginning farmers. We had little money and a mountain of debt, and our new life could be stressful and overwhelming. Harry would come over two or three times a week to pick up apple pomace (what's left after making apple cider) to feed to his cows. He only had two cows left by then, and he fed their milk to calves he raised for veal. He always wanted to hear the happenings of the day on the farm — listening closely and offering advice as I related our ups and downs.

He often came right from his egg route in Trenton, where for many years he "served" eggs to businesses and individuals. After visiting a while, he would head home with the pomace, still having to milk his cows.

Margaret was just as positive as Harry. In our early years, back when we had real winters, their long driveway would drift full of snow. I often plowed it for them. It took a long time — not so much for the plowing but because they invariably invited me in for coffee, something to eat, and a friendly chat.

We had our first Apple Day festival in 1976. My mother offered to make her apple crisp to sell at the festival — the same recipe we use in the bakery today. Pam recruited neighbors to help peel the apples. We enjoy the memory of Margaret and the kitchen knife she brought for peeling, a 12-inch butcher knife; she told us, "It's really the only knife I ever use in the kitchen."

We still have a recipe that Margaret gave Pam — a 24-hour egg soufflé. If you've ever been to a breakfast meeting here, I'm sure you've had it. The recipe is written on a 3x5 card that's creased and marked from many years of use. When Pam and I get it out to make that dish, we remember Harry and Margaret — always generous with their enthusiasm and friendship.

WHAT'S THE WEATHER?

As a farmer, the most frequent questions I'm asked are about the weather. Are your crops surviving the excess rain? Or the lack of rain? People even ask, more generally, "How does the weather affect the farm?" In lots of ways!

Farmers have a love-hate relationship with the National Weather Service, whose forecasts influence many of our day-to-day decisions: To plant, or pick, now or later. To cover crops, or not, when frost threatens. To spray before or after a predicted rain. We love the weatherman if he's right, but watch out if he's wrong.

I check the weather forecast several times a day, first on my iPhone, then my laptop. I look at weather.com (the Weather Channel), weather.org (NOAA/N.W.S.), and the Rutgers Ag Forecast (which for some reason closes shop on weekends). I've found that short-term forecasts are getting better and better — they've saved my bacon many times. Long-term forecasts aren't nearly as good. I especially like the radar map that shows the swirling clouds (color-coded for water saturation) as they move across the land.

Forecasting has come a long way since the 1960s, when Pam and I served as Peace Corps volunteers on a small Pacific island. Weathermen there, who had some of the island's few paying jobs, reported their observations four times a day over a short-wave radio. The reports were relayed again and again until they reached Guam; from there they were forwarded to a weather service center in Hawaii. Combined with reports from other parts of the Pacific, they contributed to what was then state-of-the-art forecasting.

Many of my friends on the island were navigators, a title given to those able to sail canoes to other islands — trips of 50 to 200 miles. Their ability to make accurate forecasts for the next few days (their length of time at sea) was crucial. They predicted the weather by observing the sea and sky and even the stars. Their forecasts were always spot-on.

The weather is what farmers talk about most of the time. It's too cold, too hot, too wet, or too dry. I've never met a farmer who thought the weather was just right. And this year has been extremely wet. It's mid-August and I have yet to turn on my irrigation system. My farmer friends and I are complaining that it's too wet, but when we get into a dry year, it's the same conversation in reverse. The difference is irrigation: we can add water when it's dry but can't subtract it when it's wet. Irrigating is a lot of work; it's also expensive, but the crops get the right amount of water. Farmers will always say they prefer a dry year to a wet year. But they still complain.

There are things a farmer can do in a wet year, however. I grow cherries here at Terhune Orchards. As they're ripening, heavy rains can cause them to take up too much water; they swell and crack, resulting in a ruined crop. It's a problem I've solved by installing "high tunnels" over our cherries. These are plastic, greenhouse-type structures we can erect a few weeks before harvest. We might have lost every single cherry this wet year due to cracking, but thanks to the tunnels they were perfect.

Raised beds are another way to avoid the ravages of too much rain. We now grow most of our vegetables on raised beds (mounded rows of soil); even heavy downpours aren't likely to flood the plants. Years ago, when we first started growing potatoes, we planted them in rows that weren't raised. One year, a big rain flooded our potatoes for days. All the plants died, then rotted in the field. What a smell! No wonder the Irish left Ireland during the great potato famine.

We cover many of our raised beds with black plastic. The plastic eliminates weeds, and heavy rains roll off it. Because many seeds don't germinate in saturated soil, we also use black plastic to keep beds dry until we plant them.

Sweet corn, ideally, should be planted once a week. That way, once we start harvesting, a new field is ready to pick every week. Heavy rains can disrupt this schedule, in which case I wait for a field to drain, then plant a variety that matures in 75 days while also planting my normal 85-day corn. This "catches me up," so hopefully I'll have a constant supply to pick throughout the season.

This year's excess rain hasn't affected our fruit crops much, if at all. This morning I talked with my friend Dave Duffield of Gloucester County, and we agreed that our peaches seem to have come through really well. Maybe the three H's — hazy, hot, and humid — helped us out. Sultry weather may not be fit for man nor beast, but the peaches like it just fine.

In this age of global warming, it does seem that the weather is getting more extreme. But I remember, in 1976, talking to the Mercer County agricultural agent, Charlie Holmes. One day I called him in distress about the terrible weather ruining my crops — I had just started farming and didn't know how I could continue. A few days later, Charlie stopped by to show me a horticultural publication with an article by a farmer who went into great detail about how much worse the weather was compared to the past.

After watching me read the article, nodding in agreement, Charlie pointed out the date: it was written in the 1790s! A good lesson for a young farmer to learn.

"PUTTING UP" FOR WINTER

Every spring, the first crop we harvest at Terhune Orchards is asparagus. We sell it in the Farm Store and as a pick-your-own as well. It's so great to end the winter and start our harvest! Asparagus is coming soon, and it's got me thinking about my boyhood days on our family's farm in West Windsor.

In times past, pretty much everyone "put up" food for winter. This was true of farmers, of course, but also people who grew their own vegetables and fruit in the days before supermarkets and the availability of out-of-season produce. I often get calls in January and February asking what fruit is available for picking. People see fruit in the supermarket, so why not on the farm?

Canning, freezing, drying, smoking, salting — they were all ways of preserving food for the offseason. At home on our parents' farm, we "put up" fruits and vegetables every year. I have three brothers, and feeding four hungry boys took a lot of food.

Asparagus was a favorite for all of us, my brother Lee excepted. We didn't grow asparagus but bought it from Clarence Steelman, whose farm was a few miles down Route 1, where Mercer Mall is today. Putting up asparagus was a lot of work, but we helped my mother with the job. The asparagus was blanched, then cut into pieces two or three inches long, placed into waxed paper bags, and frozen. We had a big double-door Carrier freezer in our garage, about the size of one of today's minivans. We enjoyed asparagus for dinner all winter long.

In addition to asparagus we froze sweet corn, lima beans, and green beans. Our freezer also held a winter's supply of meat — a butcher would come by the farm and cut up half a steer right in the garage.

We also put up peaches and pears — not by freezing but by "canning" in Mason jars. Oh boy, do I remember canned peaches and ice cream. We bought three-gallon tubs of ice cream delivered to us by our milkman from Decker's Dairy, in Hightstown. Three gallons didn't last long when the Mount boys were around.

(It puzzles me that my father only grew apples, along with a few pears. Back in the day, most farm families grew everything they needed. But by my father's time, the age of specialization had arrived — farmers focused on growing large quantities of just a few crops, which they marketed wholesale. By contrast, at Terhune Orchards we grow 36 crops and market them directly to our customers. Offering a wide variety of produce enhances sales.)

Another favorite dessert was our mother's cherry pies, made from sour cherries purchased from Steelman's. After bringing them home, we pitted the cherries before my mother sugared and froze them. My brothers and I did the pitting, with help from our father. The goal was freezing enough cherries to keep us in pies all winter. That took a lot of cherries, and invariably a few got past us with pits intact. Later, when eating a pie, it was exciting (if hard on the teeth) to chomp down on a pit. We brothers made a competition of it: who had the most pits in his slice of pie? Before long, more and more unpitted cherries found their way to the freezer and into our mother's pies. We never confessed to intentionally leaving any cherries unpitted, but she surely knew. It was fun placing the pits around the edge of our plates for bragging rights. My brother Bill held the record for number of pits in a slice: eight.

2014

APPLES: EAT 'EM OR DRINK 'EM

Growing up on an apple farm on Route 1 in West Windsor, I knew all I needed to know about apples: you eat them. My father's and grandfather's orchards had many varieties of apples, including many not seen today: Lobo, Turley, Ben Davis, Paragon, Transparent, Greening, Pippin, Nero, Gravenstein, the names go on and on. Whether fresh, in a pie, or as applesauce, this farm boy ate them all.

I didn't know much about consuming apples in liquid form — that is, as apple cider. Once in a while, when my father took a load of cider apples to Bob Henry's cider mill, he would bring back a few gallons. Bob, a Virginia gentleman transplanted to New Jersey, operated the mill. He didn't pronounce his name Henry, as we would. It was more like *Heyn-ree*. And it wasn't making cider, but *mekkin'* cider. The few times I saw the cider press in operation, I gloried in the intricate machinery turning apples into cider.

Fast forward 20 years later, when Pam and I bought Terhune Orchards. We decided early on that cider production and sales would be an important contributor to our farm's profits. Apples were going to be for both eating and drinking. I did not, however, know anything at all about "mekkin' cider," as Bob Henry would put it.

I was fortunate to find help in the person of George Melick of Oldwick, N.J., in Hunterdon County. Although I'd heard that George made cider, I had never met him, but when I called he graciously said to come on up to see his operation. When I got to his place, he stopped what he was doing and spent two hours showing me everything. The busier I get here on the farm, the more I have come to appreciate what a generous act this was.

Shortly before cider season, I concluded that the press and related cider-making machinery that came with the farm was out of date. Without ever having produced cider, I determined to overhaul the entire system; brash young fellow I was in those days!

Vernon Horn came over from Bucks County to help. Vernon and I worked all day and all night — right through until morning, creating a new cider mill. Vernon's assistance was the act of a good friend, and I was on my way, although my learning had just begun. It took a few years to educate myself about what apples to use and when they were ready for pressing. The first small batch I made did not sit well on the stomach of our three-year-old daughter, Reuwai: the results were disastrous! We discarded that first batch.

We've gone through many years of eating and drinking apples since 1975. Fast forward again, this time to 2010, when we made our first wine, including apple wine — yet another way to "drink" apples.

I was fortunate to find a consultant to help with this new product, Richard Carey of Lancaster, Pa. As I quickly learned, making wine is a bit more technical than making cider, and the financial consequences of producing a poor or mediocre wine at the beginning are greater.

Making apple wine involves fermentation — turning apple cider into an alcoholic drink — and to do so, we had to obtain federal and state licenses. We also had to invest in expensive equipment, but at least we had on hand plenty of the basic ingredient: apple cider. Together, my son-in-law Mike Hanewald and I have learned how to make apple wine. Now Mike pretty much does it by himself.

For the time being I've got my hands full improving and expanding our winery, but at some point down the road I'd like to start making hard cider, yet another way to "drink" apples. It's a bit trickier than making apple wine, since hard cider is a carbonated product. Which means more new machinery, and more learning for me.

TRICKLE IRRIGATION CONSERVES RESOURCES

Blueberry devotees visiting Terhune Orchards may have noticed the black plastic pipes running along the surface under our blueberry bushes. They are there to solve a watering problem that, initially, I didn't know I had.

At Terhune Orchards we don't rely on Mother Nature to provide sufficient water to the 36 crops we grow. Instead, water for irrigating is pumped from four different wells and distributed to our 200 acres of fields and orchards through a network of pipes that feed our irrigation system. The system is divided into four zones, and we can control the amount of water going to each. Most of our crops, including blueberries, rely on trickle irrigation, which delivers precise amounts of water just beneath the surface, directly to the roots.

In the summer of 1999, I noticed our blueberries weren't growing as well as they should. It was an El Niño year, meaning a dry one, and we'd been irrigating more than usual, which should have solved the problem.

What was wrong? To find out, I dug up several blueberry bushes and examined their roots. Normally, roots sense water in their immediate environment and grow toward it. Blueberry roots are very shallow, lying on or just beneath the surface. The trickle-irrigation pipes were buried a few inches below the roots, which should have grown in their direction. This year, however, we'd laid five inches of mulch around the bushes for weed control. Unexpectedly, the roots stayed put in the mulch instead of seeking the irrigation water below them. We repositioned the irrigation pipes so they ran along the surface, closer to the roots. Problem solved!

In an area like ours with dry summers that often require residents to conserve water, I try to use my irrigation water as efficiently as possible. Raised beds covered with black plastic sheeting are one way to save water. A machine pulled behind a tractor makes the beds, lays down irrigation tubes, and covers everything with the plastic, which prevents weeds from sprouting while reducing the need to water by keeping the soil moist.

Daily throughout the summer, a staff member goes through our fields and orchards, checking the soil moisture as recorded by tensiometers (tubular devices, inserted into the ground, that measure electrical resistance in the soil, a function of moisture content). We use tensiometers in pairs, one recording moisture content at 10-12 inches and the other at 20 inches. If the soil at 20 inches is dry, I give the crop a good dousing; if it's moist at 20 inches but dry at 10-12 inches, I water less.

One of the challenges of growing so many crops is juggling their diverse water requirements. Too much water for cantaloupes makes them mushy inside and tasteless, too. By contrast, tomatoes and squash thrive on generous amounts of water. Further complicating the equation, fruits and vegetables need different amounts of water at different stages in their life cycles. Those water-phobic cantaloupes, for example, need more water as seedlings than they do as mature plants.

The trickle-irrigation system that waters our blueberries and most of our other crops can also be used to supply nutrients. When the flowers in our popular cutting garden suffer from the heavy foot traffic of so many customers, I perk them up by adding liquid fertilizer to the garden's trickle-irrigation water.

Trickle irrigation isn't practical for every crop. Corn, for example, grows in tightly spaced rows covering many acres, and the cost and time to lay down literally miles of trickle-irrigation pipes would be prohibitive. Overhead sprinklers are the better option.

Sprinkler systems use much more water than trickle irrigation, and for this reason and others I limit my use of them. As noted in previous columns, in early spring I install overhead sprinklers in our strawberry fields to protect the plants from frost. An alarm system alerts me if the air temperature approaches 32 degrees so I can activate the sprinklers. (The water turns to ice, but in doing so it releases just enough energy to keep the plants from freezing.)

A trickle-irrigation system is more expensive to purchase and more complex to install and service than an overhead system, but the results — fruits and vegetables of exceptional quality — speak for themselves. Our customers concur.

2015

WEATHER

Readers of my columns know how I obsess on the topics of water and weather. Either or both can make or break a farmer's year. Water, in the form of rain, is one aspect of weather I'm able to control to some degree: in the absence of rain I can irrigate, and if it rains too much I can protect my crops from flooding by growing them on raised beds or beneath a greenhouse-like high tunnel.

As a farmer, the more I know about the weather, the better I can manage my crops. My new solar-powered weather station is a dandy. Located next to our vineyard on Van Kirk Road, it records seven weather categories: temperature, wind speed, wind direction, humidity, rainfall, leaf wetness, and solar radiation.

The weather station is linked to two forecast websites, Weather Underground (Princeton Terhune - KNJPRINC23) and Cornell University's NEWA, an important data source for practitioners, like myself, of Integrated Pest Management (I.P.M.).

As readers know, I use I.P.M. to control for codling moths, whose life cycle — from mating to egg laying to the emergence of caterpillars, which do the actual damage — proceeds according to the accumulation of degree days. Farmers have known for some time that a codling moth's eggs hatch in June — but when exactly in June? To combat codling moths, my father sprayed his apple trees five times in June. Thanks to my weather station, which tracks degree days, and its link to NEWA, I'm able to compute the exact day of caterpillar emergence and spray just once. Similar computations inform my management of peaches, grapes, potatoes, tomatoes, and other crops.

From the Roots Up

When apple growers talk about fruit, we're mainly talking about varieties. Rainier, Crimson Crisp, Pink Lady, Honeycrisp are well-known names for some really good traditional varieties. Other names are out there, too — Stayman Winesap, McIntosh, Jersey Queen. These are also excellent varieties.

All commercial apple trees are grafted trees. They're created by joining a tree's top, or scion, onto a rootstock. The scion produces apples, while the rootstock (which I think of as the tree's "engine") determines size, rate of growth, and how soon a tree starts bearing apples.

Newer rootstock varieties also control for pests and diseases. I'm glad to learn that several new varieties reportedly control for woolly apple aphids, a pest that's recently invaded my orchard.

Ditto for rootstock varieties resistant to fire blight, a particularly ravaging bacterial disease. Fire blight can infect the bark and roots of a tree and kill it fast. Last year I lost a number of apple trees from fire blight.

The names of rootstock varieties aren't nearly as evocative as the traditional apple varieties listed above; examples include M9, B9, MM111, and Geneva 11.

Roots (pronounced "ruts" by Michigan and Canadian growers) serve two purposes: they anchor a tree in the soil and take up the water and nutrients essential for growth. Some rootstocks have strong anchor roots — French crabapple especially, although it produces too large a tree for the modern orchardist.

Size control is especially important. A grower wants a uniform orchard, one that will fill the space allotted with fruitful trees. No runts, no oversized trees.

Rootstocks differ in "precocity," or tendency to bear apples early. I'm amazed to see two trees of the same variety side by side, same size and same age, but grafted onto different rootstocks. One can be full of apples and the other bare.

A grower can either purchase grafted trees or buy rootstock and the scion variety he wants to cultivate and graft them himself. There's so much demand for grafted fruit trees that suppliers can't always fulfill orders in a timely way, a problem solved by grafting your own. Usually the grafting is done in the fall; the grafted trees are then placed in a nursery for the winter and planted the following spring. But nurturing newly grafted trees is difficult, so most growers, myself included, buy their trees pre-grafted from commercial nurseries.

In a process called topworking, growers can use grafting to "swap out" one scion variety for another in the orchard. A grower does this by cutting off the old scion and replacing it with a new variety grafted onto the established rootstock. Successful topworking takes a lot of skill. Here at Terhune Orchards, the guy who does it best is Felipe Molina. We topworked some of our trees 22 years ago, when Felipe first started working for us, and he led our topworking of more trees last year.

I'm a longtime member of the International Dwarf Fruit Tree Association, which has funded rootstock research for more than 50 years. I've chaired its research committee for 25 years.

Here on the farm we also graft tomatoes and melons, whose rootstocks boost vigor, productivity, and disease resistance. Our vegetable specialist, Scott Van Kuikan, grafts our tomatoes. It's delicate, exacting work because the scion and rootstock are seedlings, just a few inches tall and quite fragile.

The next time you visit our pick-your-own apple orchard, look at a tree trunk and notice the graft callus a foot or so up from the ground. When you do, remember that it's the rootstock — the tree's "engine" — that produces the apple you love.

The Joy of Planting Trees

When Pam and I purchased Terhune Orchards 40 years ago, I had never planted an apple tree. I had grown up on an apple farm and had worked on it as a boy, but planting trees was never on my list of chores.

The apple trees that came with Terhune Orchards were old, outdated varieties. They were really big, lacked vigor, and produced poorly. A lot of effort went into growing and harvesting a crop from those monster trees. We knew right away that we had to plant new, smaller varieties. It was the real beginning of my education as an apple grower.

A few of those monster trees still survive on the farm — they're the first things you see on the right when you drive in. They date from a time when planting apples was simple compared to today. Trees came in one style 70 or 80 years ago. The rootstock was French crabapple, and the choice of varieties (the part grafted on top of the rootstock) was limited. Trees were spaced 35 by 35 feet, which allowed for 35 trees per acre. Once planted, you had to wait seven to ten years for the trees to start bearing, and 18 to 20 years for a full crop.

Today, planting apple trees is a lot more complicated. You can choose from more than 20 rootstocks. There are many more apple varieties and no end to the possible range of spacing between trees and rows. Compare the trees we found here in 1975, planted 35 trees per acre, to a recent planting of more than 2,000 trees per acre.

We planted our first apple trees in 1978, a few hundred, followed by a major planting of 10,000 trees in 1980. We've continued planting ever since — not just apples but peaches, cherries, pears, and blueberries; lots for me to think about. I love it. The best days on the farm are when we're planting trees. Whenever we plant I've made sure my children, and now my grandchildren, are there.

Four years ago, I planted eight new varieties of apples — about 4,000 trees — followed the next year with a planting of 800 peach trees. Last year we replaced 2,500 of the apples trees planted in 1980. The trees we took out were still healthy and vigorous, but the varieties had never been attractive and didn't sell very well. I think the replacement trees will do better.

Once we've planted, it's no longer a matter of wait, wait, wait. The trees are much closer together — my current favorite spacing is three feet between trees in a row and 12 feet between rows. They take a lot of care and training at first, but the trees start bearing early: we get a few apples in year two, moderate crops in years three and four, and full cropping in year five. If everything goes right, the planting reaches break-even — when it pays back the initial investment — at year nine, and we're on our way.

It's all so different from my father's day — at age 70 I'm still planting trees. Pam and I have been fortunate. Our farm, now 185 acres, is in New Jersey's Farmland Preservation Program: a commitment to permanence. Lawrence Township, our municipality, supports us, and our neighbors and customers value what we do. Most of all, we're lucky to have our daughters with us. Both are committed to farming. Tannwen has been back for 11 years, and Reuwai joined us in 2014. For farmers, that's as good as it gets.

So we continue planting trees. This year will see 700 new Stayman Winesaps, still our most popular apple, and 360 Crimson Crisps, a new variety garnering high praise from customers. We will also graft, or "topwork," 500 Enterprises, swapping them out for Crimson Crisps. The Enterprises were planted four years ago but haven't worked out. The topworking will enable us to retain the productive rootstock, and hopefully we'll be back in production in two or three years.

Planting trees begins this year around the first of April, and I hope to get my grandchildren out to help. I can't wait.

2016

OUR NEW WINERY: BUILDING A DREAM

I enjoy doing things I've never done before. Which is why I love farming — after 42 years, I'm still finding new things to do.

Building our new winery definitely falls in the category of "never done before." When our daughter Tannwen returned home after five years from California, a state with more than 4,000 wineries, she suggested we start a winery at Terhune Orchards. It didn't take much to convince me, so off we went.

We planted our first grapevines knowing it would be at least three years before we could began harvesting them. Meanwhile, we began planning the winery and learning everything we could about wine production.

There were rules and regulations we had to address, way more than I ever suspected: about wash water, septic systems, fire codes, occupancy — the list goes on. Then there was the building itself and all the wine-making equipment. Major wine-producing states like California and New York have architects who specialize in wineries, which isn't the case around here. We visited wineries in New Jersey and Pennsylvania and noted their architectural diversity — the owners had basically come up with their own designs. So that's what we did, too, in collaboration with our Amish builder's architect.

I read books about winery design and operation. They taught me some basics. I learned, above all, that a winery has to be as free of germs as possible. Floors, walls, ceilings, floor drains, lights, and other components must be cleaned on a regular basis. Even the air requires monitoring for microbes that can adversely affect wine quality.

The key to cleaning is really hot water, much hotter than the water from the faucets of a typical home. I learned this the hard way during one of our first bottlings, in 2010, when I failed to disinfect my brand new, and very expensive, Italian bottling machine — the temperature was insufficient to sterilize the bottles, resulting in a build-up of gas. I was embarrassed, to say the least, when the cork on one of our wines popped off in a customer's living room. (Fortunately, this hasn't happened since.)

Temperature is important when storing wine (55 degrees is best), and room temperature comes into play for tastings and other events. There are temperature requirements for processing wine: too cold and the yeast in the fermenting wine dies, too warm and the fermentation goes so fast that much of the flavor is lost. Our winery includes heating and air conditioning as well as a chiller to control temperature in the tanks.

My family tells me that one reason I like making wine is all the stainless steel involved. Our wine tanks and wine pumps are stainless steel; so too is the wine press, bottler, labeler, and destemmer-crusher. Wine tanks are made in the U.S. and Germany, but most come from Italy. Our 11 new Italian tanks — eight 2,000-liter, two 3,000-liter, and one 7,000-liter — arrived in two transoceanic shipping containers. Every tank is double-walled so that chilled liquid can circulate around it to keep the fermenting wine at just the right temperature.

The winery isn't quite finished, but it's progressing. The grapes are ripening, and we're racing to complete the building on time. The dream continues.

Yes, No, Maybe: The Art & Science of Pruning

Every fruit tree needs regular pruning, preferably annually. There are many opinions about pruning, and I could write many, many articles on the subject before running out of things to say. Much of what I say here about fruit trees applies equally to bushes and vines— think blueberries, raspberries, and grapes — but for simplicity's sake I'll focus mainly on trees.

The more you prune a fruit tree, the more it grows. There's a dynamic between the parts of a tree above and below ground.

During growing season, energy produced by the leaves through photosynthesis makes its way down the tree and into the roots. During winter, when branches are pruned, energy stored in the roots moves back up the tree, helping new branches to grow.

Pruning stimulates new growth and the development of appealing fruit. But what to cut? For starters, all broken or diseased branches. But some healthy branches need cutting, too. Leaves and fruit need direct sunlight to thrive, and a pruner has to consider how branches will shade each other once they've leafed out — thick with leaves, even a small branch can cast an eight-inch band of shade. Thinning distributes sunlight evenly and enhances the movement of air throughout the leaves and branches, while pruning the top of a tree directs growth out instead of up, making it easier to care for the tree and to harvest fruit (shorter trees make for shorter ladders, or no ladders at all).

So those are the basics of pruning. They're simple in theory but can be complicated and contentious in practice. Fruit growers never, ever, agree on pruning. Every winter I go to fruit growers' conferences where the subject of pruning is always addressed. The "expert" presenters never agree with each other, much to the growers' amusement (and perhaps dismay). The newer and more innovative ideas seem to generate the most disagreement. Plus you'll always find a few older guys in the back of the room muttering about dwarf fruit trees, however they're pruned: "You'll never grow anything on those bushes."

Pruning isn't a static thing. It's always changing. Last winter, I worked on a problem with our blueberries. Production and size were down, and flavor wasn't so great. I told two of our better pruners what I wanted and let them go at it while I got out of the way. (I'm better at talking about pruning than actually pruning.) The results were terrific. The bushes were more compact, and the blueberries were larger, more plentiful, and better tasting — all from pruning.

When Pam and I bought Terhune Orchards in 1975, the apple trees were 35 by 35 feet; the spacing worked out to 35 per acre, for a total of 1,000 trees — pretty big ones, too. Pruning those mammoth trees was a real chore. Today's smaller varieties have much tighter spacing — as close as 3 by 12 feet, or 1,800 trees per acre. Because the trees are so much smaller (think cornstalks), they're easier to prune, but there are many more per acre. Blueberry bushes and grapevines are planted even closer. It all adds up to a lot of pruning.

Some of the pruning is very exacting. Grapes need to be evenly spaced. At Terhune Orchards, each vine takes up six feet in a row. More or less than that isn't good. A grapevine with too much space will mature later. Too little space and it matures earlier. When harvest time approaches, all grapes look the same, and there's no way visually to tell the more mature grapes from the less mature. A wine-grape grower wants all his grapes to be equally ripe. Grapes that are over-ripe or under-ripe don't make good wine. The only way to achieve ripeness uniformity is to give each plant exactly the same space to grow. And that's the job of the pruner.

It's fall now and the weather is getting colder. It's time again to start thinking about pruning. Although the ideal month to prune in this area is March, we have so much to do we usually start in November. By "much" I mean 50,000 to 60,000 trees and plants. All pruning is done by hand, and it usually takes until April to finish.

As we get into winter, I will be planning a few trips to fruit meetings. They will include pruning demonstrations out in the orchards — even, sometimes, in deep snow. I will enjoy hearing the "experts" disagree.

It's the Berries

Yes, I'm an apple guy — apple trees, apple varieties, apple pies, you name it. But I've been thinking recently about some things much smaller and lower to the ground that make a tremendous contribution to our farm — the berry crops.

We start our season with asparagus. O.K., asparagus isn't a berry. But asparagus are soon followed by strawberries. This year we had about our best strawberry crop ever. They were large, plentiful, and tasted wonderful. This great crop came after I thought we'd lost the entire crop during three very cold nights in April. The strawberries were in bloom and temperatures went down into the low 20s. A few days after the last frost, we finally summoned the courage to pull back the covers protecting the strawberries. All the blooms were black in the center — dead. We could hardly find a live bud! I went inside and told Pam she had better stop working on her ad for *Edible Jersey* magazine — we weren't going to have any berries. But as the season progressed and Memorial Day approached, I learned how little I really knew. Miraculously, an incredible amount of berries appeared in our fields. I don't know how they survived the freeze, but it was a great crop, our best ever.

Next on our harvest list are cherries. O.K., not a berry either, but cherry harvest is followed quickly by blueberries. The past couple of years, our blueberries haven't been as good as I might have liked. They were lacking in size, flavor, and quantity. After study and consultation, the solution became clear: go back to basics. These include *weed control*: we've worked really hard at that this year. *Pollination*: I brought in extra beehives, eight in total, for our two acres of blueberries. *Irrigation and fertilization*: if soil lacks water and nutrients, the plants don't have much to work with. And finally, *pruning*: plants need meticulous trimming. Deadwood must be removed and upright canes thinned so they don't get too leggy (long). I entrusted this work to two of our staff, Kevin and Eric, who did about the best pruning job I've seen in years. The bushes are now strong and healthy, and are they loaded! I can't wait for harvest.

Blueberries are followed by blackberries. Again, it's been back to basics with weed control, fertilizer, and irrigation. Blackberries are susceptible to damage from low winter temperatures, and deadwood has to be carefully removed so new canes can grow from the bottom. It took me a while, but I've also learned the importance of protecting blackberries with bird netting. I'd been netting our blueberries for years but had convinced myself that was all the netting we needed. Then, when we started netting our blackberries two years ago, production doubled! Sometimes I wonder how we stay in business.

The last of the berry lineup are raspberries. We've grown a lot of raspberry types over the years: fall bearing, summer bearing, reds, yellows, blacks. But for various reasons we had trouble making them work with our other crops, so we haven't offered them recently. Now we're trying again. This past winter, our daughter Reuwai and I spent a lot of time looking for the right raspberry variety to fill a harvest gap in August when we don't have anything for pick-your-own. Our friends Tim and Nate Nourse of Nourse Farms, in Massachusetts, our favorite small-fruit nursery, helped us find Polana, a terrific red raspberry that's supposed to bear in August. We put in a test planting, and hopefully in a year or two we'll know how we'll finish our berry season.

SATURDAYS IN PRINCETON

I grew up on a farm on Route 1 in West Windsor, just outside of Princeton, in what was then a rural setting: not many houses near us, no other children to play with, no stores or businesses.

Lucky for me, I had three brothers. I was especially close to Lee, who was three years my senior. Lee and I kept busy on the farm. We didn't often get into trouble (at least Lee didn't), and found lots to do on our 300 acres of orchards, fields, and woods: a boy's paradise. We explored, rode our bikes (mine had fat tires; I envied Lee's skinny-tired model), and camped out. We built a dam across a drainage ditch to make a swimming hole. It worked — too well, as it turned out, flooding a section of my father's orchard. He sent some men to dismantle the dam (the job took them a while) but never reprimanded us about it.

We had plenty of ideas about things to do, and we needed stuff to do them: camping gear, tools, screws, nails, bolts, nuts. Our farm was five miles from downtown Princeton, a treasure trove for boys with a few cents in their pockets. Sometimes my mother drove us there. (With four boys in the family, someone always needed a haircut.) As we got older and more independent, we went on our own. We heard stories about my father and his brothers walking to Princeton as kids, but five miles seemed a long way. And while our parents let us ride our bikes around West Windsor, they drew the line at biking to Princeton. I'm not sure if their main concern was traffic or the possibility of university students stealing our bikes. Sometimes, though, we took the Dinky, the shuttle train between Princeton Junction and Princeton. It crossed Route 1 about a mile from our farm. We would climb the stairs from the Route 1 underpass, stand at the little station, and wave down the train when it came through. For a few cents we were in Princeton.

Our first stop was usually a hardware store. It had tools, of course, but mostly I remember the screws, nails, bolts, and nuts. We were pretty familiar with Princeton, not only for our trips to the barbershop but also our many trips to the Princeton Public Library. It was in Bainbridge House, next to the Garden Theater on Nassau Street (it's now the home of the Princeton Historical Society). Some of my earliest memories are of sitting in a special place under the stairs with a mountain of books I wanted to take home. Some 65 years later I am still a member of the library, even though as a nonresident I have to pay for being one. Well worth it, I'd say.

Back to the hardware stores. Princeton had two. One, Farr Hardware, was on Nassau Street. It was the bigger of the two and had more stuff, and the men working there were nice to us. Even so, we usually went to the other store, Urken Supply, on Witherspoon Street. Mrs. Urken had a bit of a stern reputation, but she liked the Mount boys and was always kind to us. (Her first name was Eunice, although we didn't know that at the time.) You could find anything at Urken's, and occasionally Mrs. Urkin let us go downstairs to the stockroom to find our own screws, nails, etc. That was special. Can you imagine how many screws, nails, bolts, and nuts were in those bins?

Sometimes the trip meant a stop at Hill's Market, at the corner of Witherspoon and Spring streets. My mother did her grocery shopping there, and well she might have, since my father and grandfather before him sold apples to Hill's for many years. It was a magical place that included a meat room in the back with sawdust on the floor. The clerks hurried back and forth fetching items the customers ordered. Somehow, when I went in, there was usually an open box of cookies that needed my attention. Mr. Hill still lives in the area today. I went to high school with his daughter, Janet.

Heading back up Witherspoon Street, we sometimes stopped at Princeton Clothing, where my mother bought all our "fancy" clothes. With four boys who were always hungry and growing out of their clothes, our mother was a popular lady at both Hill's Market and Princeton Clothing.

Across from Princeton Clothing was the Princeton Army-Navy Store, our source for trenching tools, mess kits, flashlights, penknives, match safes, and Army-surplus rucksacks (very heavy). Anything we couldn't afford we requested for Christmas. My brothers and I were Boy Scouts. We liked to hike and camp, and the Army-Navy Store met all our needs for our busy outdoor lives. I recently spoke with the owner, Michael Bonin, a few days before the store finally closed its doors for good. I had known his father, Al, and am old enough to remember his grandfather Joe.

My brothers and I worked on the farm Saturday mornings, but our Saturday afternoons were usually free. We sometimes earned our "going to Princeton" money raking brush, using a pitchfork to pile apple prunings in the space between rows for chopping up. We also fixed apple boxes for five cents apiece. Apple farms now use 20-bushel bins to store their apples, but back then they were stored in one-bushel boxes.

Sometimes we hailed the Dinky and rode it into town with our bikes, which we then pedaled to another favorite place, Kopps Cyclery, on Spring Street. After buying whatever parts or accessories we needed, we pedaled back to the Dinky Station and took the train home. As the Dinky approached our farm we had to speak up quickly, otherwise the conductor continued on to Princeton Junction and we had to pedal home from there.

We always looked forward to our Saturdays in Princeton for everything the town provided for our busy lives on the farm — especially all those screws, nails, bolts, and nuts.

2017

CRUSHING GRAPES

This year marks the second "crush" for the new Terhune Winery. "Crush" is a term for the initial steps of turning grapes into wine, from destemming to placing the grapes in a wine tank to ferment. In the fall of 2016, when we did our first crush, the winery building was still under construction. The 11 stainless-steel wine tanks shipped to us from Italy were on site but had yet to be installed, and we couldn't do the crush without them. When I told our builder, Sylvan Stoltzfus, that we needed the tanks in place now, before the building was ready for them, he objected: "Gary, you just cannot do that!" It took some effort to convince him otherwise and to erect the tanks in the unfinished space. We also had to convince township officials to issue us a temporary certificate of occupancy. Despite the obstacles, our 2016 crop made it safely into the tanks.

We figured that this year, with the completed winery up and operating, the crush would be a cinch. Not so.

It started with the harvest. Throughout the preceding year we had put a lot of effort into nurturing the grape crop. We took care to combat powdery mildew, downy mildew, black rot, botrytis, and sour rot. We carefully pruned in winter and kept the growing shoots neatly tucked into the trellis throughout the summer. We removed most of the leaves around the grape clusters to better expose them to the sun and reduce disease. Believe me, there are a lot of leaves in nine acres of grapes.

At harvest time we tested each grape variety repeatedly — trying to find the exact right time to pick. Sugars needed to be high enough, acidity needed to be in balance, and we needed to avoid rainstorms just before picking. Our efforts proceeded in an orderly fashion, just as expected. Then things got complicated. The grape harvest arrived in the middle of our apple harvest. I anticipated this and thought it would be easy to switch from apples to grapes and back, but I failed to appreciate the time it would take — we had an exceptional crop of both apples and grapes. We also had to prepare for our fall harvest festivals. We have a great crew of skilled workers, but moving quickly from task to task was still a challenge.

Once grapes are harvested, processing begins immediately. Grapes for white wines are removed from the stems, slightly crushed, and then pressed to separate the juice from the skins and seeds. The juice then goes into the tank for fermentation. Grapes for red wines are removed from the stems and then go directly into the tank and pressed after fermentation.

We're fortunate to have Tony McDonnell working for us. Tony, who is taking an online wine course from Washington State University, checks the sugars and acid levels, adds yeasts, and keeps track of what's happening in each of the 11 tanks. The tanks range in size from 2,000 to 6,800 liters — that's 528 to 1,899 gallons. It's a big job. We also have Adrian, Johnny, Austin, and Kevin helping us. With so much activity — even with such great employees — we find that we can't do any processing on festival weekends. The scheduling of festival preparation, apple harvest, and grape harvest is complicated by the demand that we finish the week's grape harvest on Thursday. Friday is for crushing and pressing. The festivals take place Saturday and Sunday.

All summed up, our 2017 crush went well. The grape quality was good, we were able to get the grapes picked and crushed on time, and we had enough tank space to store all the wine. We purchased a new wine press — larger and with the latest technology; given its price, only a wine maker could love it. Some of the wines will be bottled next spring as we empty the tanks for next year's crush.

PICK, PICK, PICK

Selling produce directly to customers on the farm where it's grown is a relatively new concept in farming. When I was growing up on my family's farm in West Windsor, farmers generally sent their produce to wholesale distribution centers or straight to stores. The idea of selling to customers at your own farm store or allowing them to buy what they picked in the field, like we've done for many years at Terhune Orchards, was limited. (Farmers did sell their produce at local or regional farmers markets. The Trenton Farmers Market dates from the 1920s, and we've been a member for many years.)

"Pick-your-own" came into its own in the 1960s, when families were larger and many households still "put up" summer produce for winter by canning and freezing. Because the price per pound of self-picked produce was less than what they would pay for it in the store, families could purchase large quantities of produce at lower cost. Farmers benefited from the larger volume sold and by having to hire fewer farm laborers to do their picking. Pam and I remember the days of bigger families — they bought a lot of produce! We especially liked families with teenagers because teens are always hungry.

This phase of pick-your-own peaked in the 1970s, then declined due to the decreasing size of families and the increasing number of households in which both spouses worked (the wife wasn't home to do all that canning and freezing).

In recent years, pick-your-own has enjoyed a renaissance. Customers want to see up close where and how their food is grown, and they like selecting it themselves, fresh off the tree, bush, or plant. Parents also want to show their kids where food actually comes from — that it's not grown in a supermarket.

Pick-your-own does have its challenges. Some fruits are fragile and easily damaged when picked by untrained pickers. Some have short harvest windows: they can be under-ripe one weekend and over-ripe the next. And some are so popular — our cherries, for example — that demand exceeds supply: they're "picked out" early, to the dismay of customers who miss out on the picking.

Another challenge is the changing size of our apple trees. In our first pick-your-own orchard we limited tree height to six and a half feet so all apples could be reached from the ground. Now, as we gradually replant with newer (and better) varieties, we're growing taller trees for increased production. So how will our customers reach the apples at the top? A few of my apple-grower friends have offered suggestions, and when you visit this year you may see something new in picking.

Regardless, our beautiful apples will be here — one of our best crops ever — so you can pick, pick, pick.

ENERGY AT TERHUNE: WE'VE GOT THE POWER!

I was inspired to write this article when we finished the solar installation on our new wine barn. It got me thinking about electric power on the farm over the years.

Pam and I have been here 42 years, but the farm had power long before then. The first (mechanical) power came from a windmill located over a hand-excavated well 20 feet from the farmhouse. Installed in the early 1900s, it pumped water for the house and livestock and saved a lot of labor. The windmill pumped water but didn't generate electricity, so the farm continued to rely on kerosene lamps for lighting. This was the norm; in 1920 only 10 percent of the nation's farms had electricity.

(After the windmill was built, I wonder if the Terhune family had trouble adjusting to the noisy blades and gearbox? I grew up in a farmhouse on Route 1. Then as now, heavy truck traffic on that busy thoroughfare generated a lot of noise, but because it was constant I scarcely noticed. When our family moved into a new house farther from the highway, at first we had trouble sleeping — the nights were too quiet!)

I learned about early power on the farm from Charles Hunt, a Terhune son-in-law, and Dick Terhune, the son of Stanley Terhune, who owned the farm from the 1920s through the 1940s. They recalled how, at some point, the windmill was adapted to turn a generator, which produced direct current that charged a set of batteries; the generator and batteries were part of a unit built by Delco and marketed to farmers. Wires from the batteries distributed current to the barn (to power electric lights — cows were milked twice a day, often before sunup), and to the farmhouse, where it was used for lighting and to run a wringer-type clothes washer. Although a marked improvement over kerosine lamps, the electric lights were limited by battery capacity. Elsie Terhune Davison, who with her husband, Jack, sold us the farm, told me, "When the batteries wore down, we went to bed."

(Some farms relied on diesel-powered generators for electricity. In his farming memoir *Gleanings from the Past*, my friend Charles Grayson of Belle Mead describes his father's 32-volt Fairbanks Morse Light Plant, whose diesel engine charged two 16-volt Leyden glass-jar batteries.)

The next big leap in the farm's electrification was connecting to the grid. Dick Terhune recalled that the power company asked his father to pay for the five utility poles and wiring needed to bring electricity up Cold Soil Road from Carter Road; the poles cost $40 each. (Such a request wasn't unusual. Utilities also asked farmers to install electric stoves to assure enough power was consumed to return a profit.) The Terhunes rewired their washing machine to run on the grid's alternating current. The cost of running the washer was 12 cents a month. I don't recall the cost when we bought the farm in 1975, but it was surely more.

The electricity from the grid was originally single phase (three wires), which is suitable for small motors and lighting. Higher-voltage three-phase power (four wires), which is better for large motors and refrigeration, came along later, but it's expensive. In 1985 it would have cost us $50,000 to extend three-phase power lines from Carter Road. Fortunately, the neighbor up from us needed three-phase power and paid to have the lines installed. We now have three separate three-phase services — for our wells, winery, and apple cold-storage rooms — as well as two diesel-powered emergency generators to get us through the occasional power failure.

Our new solar installation is slightly smaller than an earlier system we installed in 2010 (33 vs. 39 kilowatts) but costs about half as much to operate: solar equipment prices have dropped, and design and efficiency have improved. The solar power supplements the "high-line" three-phase power used in our winery and cold storage — we hope to the tune of 30 to 40 percent. The solar panels generate direct current, just like the Delco wind generator of a century ago, but our system includes an inverter that changes the direct current to three-phase alternating current.

When you visit the farm I'd be glad to show you all this. We've got the power!

2018

FARMLAND PRESERVATION II

When Pam and I purchased Terhune Orchards in 1975, the idea of permanence — keeping the farm available for farming for future generations — was not our primary goal. Our immediate goals were to get the farm going, make it productive and profitable, and have enough money left over for the mortgage payments (enormous to us in those days).

Thinking back on those days, I wish we'd focused on permanence right from the start. My experience with the loss of my father's farm in West Windsor was a reminder of the impermanence of agriculture in New Jersey.

Farming in most of New Jersey is a less profitable use of land than developing it for commercial or residential space (e.g. office complexes, malls, or housing tracts). In my father's day, farm properties were assessed not for their value as farmland but for their potential value to developers. This led my father and his brothers to sell the family farm in 1961 rather than passing it on to their children and burden them with an inheritance tax they'd be unable to pay.

The N.J. Department of Agriculture, along with the state Farm Bureau and supporting farm groups, addressed this issue, proposing legislation that led to passage of the Farmland Assessment Act of 1964, which permits farmland to be assessed by its productivity, not by what a developer might be willing to pay for it.

Although an important first step, the act failed to address the core issue of long-term farmland preservation — in places with rapid population and commercial growth, farmers still had an incentive to sell out to developers. Along with a farmland *assessment* act, we needed a farmland *preservation* act that would provide farmers incentives to set aside their properties forever.

My friend Sam Hamill headed New Jersey Future, a planning group, and was a passionate advocate for farmland preservation. Sam saw a way forward and recruited me — young, big-bearded, tieless — to help. Along with representatives from the Department of Agriculture and Farm Bureau, we held a series of seminars, toured state-preserved farmland in Maryland, and organized a conference at the RCA/Sarnoff research center in Princeton.

It was a grassroots effort that culminated in passage of the Farmland Preservation Act of 1982. Under terms of the act, landowners who wish to continue farming their land can sell their development rights to the state, to their municipality or County Agriculture Development Board, or to a nonprofit group. The sale price is based on the difference between the land's potential to a developer and its value for agriculture. Deed restrictions limit future use of the land to farming, in perpetuity.

To date, close to $2 billion has been spent to permanently preserve more than 233,000 acres of New Jersey farmland, a third of all land now farmed in the state. We are deeply indebted to visionaries like Sam, former Secretary of Agriculture Art Brown, and the many farmers, farm groups, and farming advocates for making the program a success.

The four farms comprising Terhune Orchards are all enrolled in the state's farmland preservation program, which has made it easier for our daughters, Reuwai and Tannwen, to look forward to a future in farming. They have both joined us in our farm business and were adamant that we preserve the last of the four farms, our 26-acre pick-your-own apple orchard.

They love Terhune Orchards, as do their children. Our 10-year-old grandson recently said, "This is going to be *my* farm someday." And our three granddaughters tell us "how lucky we are to grow up on a farm." Pam and I are lucky, too.

So You Want to Be a Farmer?

Hold on to your hats! It's a Terhune first. After 40 years of *Terhune Orchards News*, this is the first-ever combined Pan and Gary column. But really, we could only write this one together, because it's our story.

* *

PAM: Gary and I are often asked how we came by the idea of owning and running a fruit and vegetable farm. It's a long story, but if you, too, have wondered, here goes. The story starts right here in Princeton.

I lived just off Terhune Road in Princeton with my family. Gary grew up in West Windsor on his family farm on Route 1, which was sold in the early '60s. We started dating when I was a senior at

Princeton High School and he was a freshman at Princeton University. I went off to Ohio for college. Three days after I graduated in 1967, we were married, and three months later we joined the newly formed Peace Corps and took off to Micronesia, which we knew nothing about except it covered a big piece of the Pacific Ocean. After training on Truk Island and staying for a while on Yap Island, we settled on Satawal, a very small island, a mile long and half-mile wide in the western Caroline Islands, three degrees above the equator. We spent three enchanting, challenging, and rewarding years with the 400 islanders living there.

Satawal is known for the fantastic master navigators who sail the open ocean in handmade outrigger canoes using information passed down from father to son. Stars, waves, currents — all tell them where the canoe is located in the vast blue ocean.

Once we learned the local language, we were totally engaged in the life of the island. I taught the children English and other subjects and helped organize lessons for the three local teachers. The head teacher had the equivalent of a third-grade education under the Japanese occupation prior to World War II. So there was a lot to organize.

GARY: I became an agricultural agent, providing assistance in coconut production. I had grown up on a farm but was not a farmer (yet). I had wanted to go to agricultural school (Cornell, Penn State, Rutgers) and join my father on his farm. However, when he found out that I could get into Princeton, the matter was settled. I had to go there, and if I wanted to farm I "could always pick that up later." Fortunately for the Satawalese, I had some farming knowledge. I brought in new, better varieties of coconuts and helped replant half of the island's groves. (This must have worked out well because the islanders later replanted the other half.) I supervised the building of a 20,000-gallon water catchment (still in use today, 50 years later, and expanded by the islanders), and I helped build dryers to facilitate the sale of the island's only cash crop, coconuts. I was doing much of the same type of work I've done for the past 43 years at Terhune Orchards.

PAM: In 1970 we left the Peace Corps and traveled home slowly, visiting much of the world from the Pacific eastward. Returning to the Princeton area, we tried to settle in. Our first daughter, Reuwai, was born in 1972. By 1975 we were restless.

It so happened that on the end of the driveway at 330 Cold Soil Road we saw a sign saying, "For sale by owner." We began talking to the owners of Terhune. They never imagined selling their small farm would be to people who wanted to farm, and we didn't realize that no one had bought farmland for farming in Mercer County for 20 years. Development was the name of the game.

But we really wanted to try re-creating the same sense of community we had found at Satawal. Starting with the original 55 acres of huge apple trees, run-down barns and house, no equipment, no irrigation, and no help. I was also pregnant with our second daughter, Tannwen. No problem! Once we convinced banks to loan us enough money we finally completed the purchase in March 1975. Now we were off and running.

The farm had enjoyed a small, local following August to September, having set up an old barn to sell apples, peaches, and cider. Half of the people we met thought we were two crazy young people who would go out of business in short order. The other half were wonderfully encouraging and believed we would somehow make it all work. Thank goodness for them!

We read a lot, asked a lot of questions, went to all the agricultural conferences, and joined all the agricultural groups. Since we really didn't know what we were doing, we tried out all kinds of creative ideas. Most of them worked! Our son, Mark, joined the family in 1978.

In the 1980s we were able to buy a 27-acre farm on Van Kirk Road for planting a modern pick-your-own apple orchard.

GARY: I like taking on things I haven't done before and ideas not many others have tried. Sometimes it works out — happily, more often than not. The new orchard was an example. No one had ever planted a high-density apple orchard in our area. The 12,000 trees I planted on 26 acres were more than my father had on his entire 250 acres! Challenges of financing, irrigation, tree support, purchasing compatible equipment for the narrow rows — I loved it all. A lot of the solutions had to be "home grown" or researched from what was done in orchards far away.

PAM: At first, not that many people wanted to pick their own, so we picked the apples and sold them in the Farm Store.

One of the big challenges was how to get people to come out to the farm! Most people were used to shopping at the supermarket. Since we didn't have the resources to use paid advertising, we started having festivals and events, inviting the public to join us on our farm. It was fun — and still is! Soon we had our own store open every day and year-round. Our children grew out of the apple boxes they played in as babies, and as our family grew, so did the families that came to Terhune Orchards. Now we have three and sometimes four generations of families visiting and enjoying all the activities that memories are made of on our farm.

GARY: Our friends find it curious that we thrive on thousands of people visiting us each year. They don't know the back story, which is that when we started out, Pam thought we should create a commune! Unfortunately for her dreams, I wanted to be someone you don't generally find on a commune: the boss. So Pam brought the commune to the farm: she invited the whole community (sometimes I think it's the whole world) to join us. It's been great.

We like growing things on our farm and selling them to our thousands of customers. I don't think I'd be as happy providing a service, but producing something tangible is very satisfying. Farmers most always live on their farms, and much of the time farming is a husband-and-wife cooperative enterprise — this was so important to us after working together our first three married years on joint projects in the Peace Corps. Finally, there are the farm children. I'm so grateful to have had a job where I could see my children grow up — to be with my family every day. We spend our time at Terhune Orchards working every day of the week, but when it comes to an event in our children's (and now grandchildren's) lives, we're able to be there — we can find the time to go. Many, many thanks to our friends and customers who support us and this farm.

It's for the Birds

When Pam and I bought Terhune Orchards 43 years ago, I had many preconceptions of the challenges we would encounter as farmers. Finances, of course (we had no money), government regulations, marketing our crops, disease and insect problems — I thought I knew. I never suspected that our biggest challenge would be animals and birds devouring our crops. Deer are really tough — I will write about them someday. Raccoons, ground hogs, and squirrels are out there on the farm every day, munching away. But the worst, the absolutely most distressing, are birds.

We're fruit growers, which means there's nothing we grow that birds don't like. They are, as our longtime employee Emiliano Martinez said, "our partners." We started our first season with just three main crops (apples, peaches, and pears), plus whatever we could harvest from four cherry trees.

Cherries were our first crop of the season. The previous owner said he never harvested any cherries because the birds ate them all, but I was determined. I found two old carbide cannons in the barn and was able to get them to work. The cannons made a loud noise to scare away birds. They worked by dripping water onto a block of calcium carbide, producing acetylene gas. As the gas rapidly accumulated it expanded into the firing chamber while setting off a spark from a device resembling a cigarette lighter. The resulting explosion scattered every bird in sight, at least for a while.

The explosions continued throughout the day, and before too long we began to "meet" our "neighbors," some of whom lived three miles away: those carbide cannons were loud.
Car after car pulled into the drive. Some of the folks were understanding — they got it that we were just trying to protect our crop — and some were not. If only we could attract that many customers to buy our cherries!

Soon enough, the birds got used to the noise, even if our neighbors didn't. The cannons worked for a few days, at best, before the birds returned and stayed. Also, I had to fuss with the cannons to keep them working, and if I forgot to shut them off at night . . . then I really got to "meet" the neighbors.

The carbide cannons went back into the barn. We bought bird netting and struggled to get it over our 15-foot-high cherry trees. When the cherries were ready, we hired high school kids to pick them.

Such excitement — our first crop ever. We "made" $40, a figure that excludes the several hundred dollars we spent on netting and harvest labor. We took the cash and went out to dinner. In the years since, we've done a bit better than $40 on our cherries, but the birds have remained our adversaries.

Our next crop was peaches. Unfortunately, our main peach orchard was on rented land right next to where a neighboring farmer kept his corn in corncribs. The wire mesh on the corncribs was in bad repair. Great flocks of birds of several types feasted on his stored corn, then flew out to our peach orchard for dessert. Crows would eat half a peach at a time. Blue jays, greedy creatures that they are, would give one quick peck — ruining the peach — then move on to another. Smaller birds like starlings just ate and ate.

Soon after our children started school they were bringing home bird feeders they'd made in shop class. Worried that placing the feeders around the house would attract even more birds, I said no to the feeders. Years later, I counted ten bird feeders stored on shelves just inside our back door. My poor kids.

When we started planting blueberries, two acres initially, I learned more about bird damage. In southern New Jersey, where thousands of acres of blueberries are grown, two acres lost to birds isn't so serious. For us, that's a 100-percent loss! And birds *love* blueberries. I decided to repel them with an electronic bird-scaring device that works by broadcasting distress and predator calls at intervals throughout the day. When I first installed the device and turned it on, the birds rose from the blueberry patch in a thick black swarm: very impressive.

Our problem wasn't solved, however. It was almost biblical — on the seventh day the birds returned. They no longer feared the electronic squawks and shrieks. So we went back to nets. We bought two acres of netting; it took three days to erect a two-acre netting tent that reached all the way to the ground on all sides. We finished and happily stood on the porch of the Farm Store and admired the net in all its glory. Perfect, we thought. But less than an hour after we'd installed the net, a thunderstorm swept in and blew it into rows of tomatoes we were growing on four-foot cages. What a mess.

I'm not a patient person. Stubborn, yes, but patient, no. I can't even deal with tangled kite string or fishing line. Our employees convinced me to find something else to do while they painstakingly reconstructed the net.

Since then, we've been growing more "dessert" items for birds. More cherries, as well as blackberries and both table and wine grapes. We've adopted a netting system called "Smartnet" from British Columbia and have gotten better at keeping out the birds. Pretty successfully, in fact — at least if you discount the time we failed to retract the wine-grape net soon enough to avoid a Halloween snowstorm. Not even our meticulous employees could fix that one, and 5.5 acres of bird netting ended up in the dumpster.

Grapes are extra-special delicious to birds, especially to crows. Last year, we ran short of netting and had to leave two rows of grapes uncovered until more netting we ordered arrived. By that time, every grape on the two rows was gone — stripped right off. We finished installing the net, buttoned everything up, and went on to other jobs. A week later, an employee reported that a crow had found its way inside the net. I sent several of our guys to deal with it. When they didn't return and I went to investigate, I found them chasing the crow inside the net while a hawk flew just outside and above the net, tracking the crow back and forth as it fled its arm-waving pursuers. I realized that crows are a lot more afraid of hawks than they are of humans. I'm now looking for ways to encourage more hawks to live near our fields.

Sometimes, if we succeed in keeping birds out of one crop, they switch to another. This past year birds attacked our cantaloupes and watermelons. On the first day, while we went for our 30-minute lunch, they destroyed over 300 melons!

To deal with the melon threat we turned to an old-fashioned method: scarecrows. Pam had been making scarecrows for years, but just for show. (We placed them in front of our house, where they greeted customers.) She made the first of our scarecrows intended to actually "scare crows," then invited employees to make more. We placed a total of seven scarecrows out in the melon field, and the crows and other birds stayed away. When the birds got used to the scarecrows and began returning to the field, we found that moving the scarecrows around scared them anew. We also stretched flashy ribbon all over the field. Everything helped, and we wound up with a successful crop of melons. Still, I find it hard to believe one of my biggest farming challenges is "for the birds."

VARIETY: THE SPICE OF LIFE

I'm writing this while returning from an apple growers' trip to New Zealand. One of the things I do is travel the world with other apple growers, looking at orchards. Annually, we visit and analyze apple orchards in the U.S. and abroad. This year's trip took us to the southern hemisphere, where we saw not only orchards, but apples, and lots of them: it's harvest time in New Zealand. We looked at the apple trees themselves, taking note of their height, width, spacing between trees and rows, and rootstocks. All sorts of fascinating things, at least to an apple grower. Our visit offered an additional treat: many new apple varieties. Whether we're talking about fruits or vegetables, varieties add spice to a farmer's life. Varieties can differ in taste, color, shape, size, firmness, keeping qualities, texture — the list goes on. In the apple business, especially New Zealand's export apple business, a desirable variety can make the difference between an orchard's success or failure.

New Zealanders (Kiwis) are leaders in developing new apple varieties. They find some by means of controlled cross breeding of two known varieties: the pollen of one apple is used to fertilize the flower of another apple. Usually this is done with a camel-hair brush. The seeds of the resulting apple are planted, and the new trees are carefully observed. It's a slow, exacting process, which with luck can result in a great new apple variety. Other varieties result from the natural mutation of a fruit bud or tree limb. Usually this happens in the orchard of a sharp-eyed grower who spots the mutation and is smart enough to keep it when pruning the following winter. After a year or two of observation, the grower contacts a nursery about propagating the new variety.

New apples we saw had names like Galaxy, Smitten, Rockit, and Piqua-Boo. We decided that Kiwis are better at growing apples than naming them.

Our apple growers' group, the International Fruit Tree Association (IFTA), last visited New Zealand 18 years ago. New Zealand has a small population and exports almost all its apples, traditionally to Great Britain. During our previous visit, New Zealand mainly exported Cox's Orange Pippen, a favorite of Brits but not so marketable to anyone else (taste buds are regional). Kiwi growers were in trouble: Great Britain had joined the European Union, and lower-cost apples from France and Germany had flooded the U.K. market, leaving the Kiwis with apples that were difficult to sell elsewhere in the world. In the last 20 years, the Kiwis have rebuilt their industry by breeding and developing new varieties appealing to the tastes of Asian countries closer to home. Chinese, Koreans, Japanese, and Vietnamese consumers like their apples large, red, and very sweet.

As orchards were replanted, New Zealanders adopted new techniques and rootstocks. They learned to use their abundant sunshine and long growing season to best advantage. Their shipping and marketing systems are tops. The quality of their apples is excellent, and production and profits are high.

Many of their new ideas came from IFTA, which over the past 60 years has been steadfast in the free exchange of information. We fund research in better apple growing (I'm chair of the research committee) and hold annual conferences at fruit-growing locations around the world. As visitors, we were met by friendly Kiwi fruit growers. We share a common passion, and our histories have been their histories.

* * *

And then there's the coconut. On the way home from New Zealand, Pam and I stopped in Hawaii to see Mike and Angelina McCoy. Our connection with Mike goes back 50 years, when we served as Peace Corps volunteers on Satawal, an island in Micronesia smaller than my father's farm in West Windsor. Pam and Mike were teachers; I was an agricultural agent. I specialized in coconut culture — important because coconuts were the island's life-sustaining crop. The islanders wanted help developing new varieties.

Satawal coconuts were small. When husked, the nut was about the size of a tennis ball. I was able to introduce a new variety that was not only a good growing plant, but had a much larger coconut. When husked, the nuts were bigger than a large grapefruit. We set the nuts, which are really coconut seeds, out in a nursery, and when they sprouted, we planted the best-looking ones.

During our time on Satawal we replanted about half of the island with the new variety. Our three years in the Peace Corps ended before I saw the results of my labors. When Pam and I returned to the island 20 years ago (one week of travel in each direction — it's still remote), it was a memorable and moving visit that included our attending the ordination of one of Pam's students as a Catholic priest. Another highlight was realizing what I'd accomplished as a coconut breeder. As the trees I had planted matured, the Satawalese had taken the nuts and replanted the rest of the island. One of my happiest moments ever was overhearing a visitor from another island ask, "Where did the Satawalese get such large coconuts?"

We had a wonderful visit with Mike and Angie in Hawaii. As we headed home on the last leg of our journey, I started thinking about the work ahead at Terhune Orchards. One of our first crops for picking will be strawberries, and I need to get them uncovered, weeded, and fertilized. Later this year we will plant a new strawberry field with a terrific new variety, Rutgers Scarlet. It has big berries, nicely red and with outstanding taste. They'll be ready to pick in May of 2019. New varieties: the spice of this grower's life.

2019

OH, DEER!

During my 45 years of farming, among the most serious challenges I've faced are wild animals that eat what we grow. They include birds, racoons, ground hogs, mice, and voles. But the worst of all are deer.

Deer were rarely seen when I was a kid growing up on an apple farm near Princeton. If deer were sighted in the orchard, it was an event, and my father would tell us about it at dinner. There just weren't that many deer in New Jersey. Now, the state's deer population is tremendous, and deer damage makes it almost impossible to farm successfully, especially if you're growing fruits and vegetables. Deer love to eat every crop I grow, especially apples. They eat the apples and leaves of our trees during the growing season. They rub the bark from the trunks with their antlers in fall and eat the fruit buds in winter. (Can you imagine how many fruit buds it takes to fill the stomach of a hungry deer?)

I've been battling deer since we bought Terhune Orchards in 1975. I started with repellents, which I sprayed on the trees. This worked for a while, until rain washed off the repellent and it was dinner time again. I've also hung natural repellents in small mesh bags tied to the branches; the repellants included human hair (men's hair only — women's hair is washed before cutting) and blood meal. For a while I was buying so many 2-by-3-inch bags from Flemington Bag and Burlap Company I became a "person of interest" to the federal drug agents. I explained to them what I was doing, but they weren't immediately convinced.

Repellents worked at first, but between the rain and the adaptability of deer, they eventually lost their effectiveness.

Fencing followed. I tried building a fence around each small tree, but when planting 500 to 1,000 trees per acre, that was ridiculous. I also noticed that when the small trees got bigger, the deer would stand on their hind legs and jump. They could snatch apples 10 to 12 feet off the ground.

A friend suggested I get a state permit to shoot the deer. That hasn't worked here or anywhere else in the state. I work all day, seven days a week, and am way too tired to sit out in our orchards in the evening and early morning to shoot deer.

Besides, my farmer friends who have tried shooting deer say they can't shoot enough of them to make a difference. New Jersey's sport hunters kill 40,000 deer a year, while deer-car collisions kill 50,000 more. That accounts for close to 100,000 deer a year, but the population keeps growing. The N.J. Farm Bureau counts deer herds using night-flying drones with infrared cameras. Its aerial surveys show 300 to 400 deer per square mile in parts of Warren County; biologists say the optimal number is 15 per square mile.

Back to fencing: I next tried electric fencing around the farms. It was four to five feet high, with four or five electrified wires, similar to what stockmen use for their pastures. This worked well at first, but then, as they always do, the deer adapted. They lost their fear of the fence. The deer learned they could jump straight through the fence without being shocked so long as their feet didn't touch the ground. They learned to crawl under the fence without touching it. Electric fencing kept some deer out, but as one of our employees told me, I still had my "partners" out in the field every night. I've resorted to a barrier-type, woven-wire fence around the farm. Pam calls it the "penitentiary" look. It costs a lot to fence in four farms totaling nearly 200 acres. Through tria l and error we've learned the best way to build the fence: no gaps more than six inches at the bottom; use high-tensile wire, which springs back into place after removing a fallen tree; keep the gate closed at night.

For the time being at least, the deer are no longer my "partners." I've found I can cut back my plantings of a particular vegetable and still have enough, even when I plant only 50 percent of what I did for the partnership.

WINTER WORK II

I've written about farmers' winter work before, but in the last few years it's changed some, so time for an update.

Our outdoor winter work begins with covering strawberries. We've been planting strawberries in the summer, cropping them for two years, then replanting. To increase productivity we're now trying to replant annually, which means planting in the fall and harvesting in May. Whether we replant annually or biannually, leaving strawberry plants exposed to cold, dry winter winds leads to a lot of damage. So we cover them with a woven synthetic fabric, 9 ounces per square yard, that comes in rolls 50 by 800 feet. It's quite a bit of work getting our four to five acres of strawberries covered each year.

Early winter work also includes removing the black plastic "mulch" we use on many of our vegetables — squash, melons, herbs, tomatoes, peppers, and broccoli. All are grown on black plastic, which warms the soil and keeps weeds in check. In early winter, our first job is removing the plastic and taking it from the field.

Pruning, that exacting art and science, remains our biggest winter chore. All fruit crops need pruning. Every tree and every bush, every year. Pruning removes old low-vigor, broken, diseased, or shaded branches. They have to go to make way for the new. Younger branches bear more and larger fruit that looks and tastes better.

Pruning continues all winter. The employees doing it have skills that come from long experience. Pruning makes any plant less winter hardy, so we prune the hardier trees — apples and pears — first. (We have 35,000 to 40,000 apple trees, so we would need a head start on them anyway.) Peach trees (3,000) and cherry trees (1,000) are less winter hardy, so we wait until mid to late February for them.

Blueberry bushes (3,000) are winter hardy, so whether we prune them early or late isn't critical. Whenever we do, it's important to remove enough of the old canes to allow the younger ones room to grow. I can't bear doing this myself, and don't even try. Instead, I wait for our trusted employee Kevin Francis to return from his annual vacation in his native Jamaica. He and I discuss what needs to be done, and he goes to it.

In recent years we've added grapevines to our winter pruning list. Pruning grapevines is tricky: prune too much and vines tend toward vigorous growth, which isn't ideal for plentiful and flavorful fruiting. Prune too little and vines lose vigor, are less productive, and grape quality declines.

All fruits should be picked when they reach maturity. You can tell when to pick apples, peaches, and cherries by their color. Not so with grapes — they turn color well before they're ready for picking. We have methods for testing grapes for maturity but can't test every vine. Instead, we rely on pruning to keep the vines uniform — if one vine in a row is mature we know the others are, too. It's winter pruning that keeps the grape vines uniform: no big, bushy vines and no starved-looking, runty ones, either. Vines are planted six feet apart, and the pruning staff trains each vine to just fill its space.

(Sometimes it isn't enough just to prune. This year we removed all of our unproductive grapevines: those that were sick, winter-damaged, or virus-infected; also, varieties that grew poorly or lacked flavor. Last year we did a similar culling of our apple trees.)

The vineyard is a new part of Terhune Orchards, as is the winery. Grape harvesting and fermenting take place in the fall; in winter comes filtering, blending, and bottling. As noted, you need good grapes of optimum maturity to make good wine. You also need clean equipment. Our winter work in the winery begins and ends with cleaning. We clean everything, from the drains in the floor to the wine tanks themselves to the HVAC in the ceiling. We circulate cleaning solution through all the hoses and blast the bottling machine with a 20-minute steam bath.

We try to schedule bottling — the final stage of wine production — for bad-weather days so outside workers (pruners) can help with it. Otherwise, we want to keep them in the field doing their winter work, which has to be finished before spring arrives.

Wine Maker's Dreams

Wine making has opened a whole new world for me. My life has always been connected to farming — that is, growing something. I grew up on a farm near Princeton, and then I became an agricultural advisor in the Peace Corps; coconut culture was my specialty. I've been farming at Terhune Orchards now for 25 years. With all that experience, you might think there aren't that many new things to learn. Not so.

I love growing grapes and making wine because so much of it is new to me. We make a lot of wine from our apples, blueberries, and peaches, but most of it is made from grapes. When it comes to growing and processing grapes, I'm still low on the learning curve. Wine makers have a saying, "It's easy to make bad wine from good grapes but very hard to make good wine from bad grapes."

Growing good grapes is a must, but grapes are touchy. I used to think growing peaches was difficult — insects and diseases can ravage them — but peaches are easy compared to grapes. Black rot, phomopsis, botrytis, powdery mildew, and downy mildew are just a few of the many grape diseases. They're each classified as a fungus. New Jersey's hot, muggy, wet weather is a delight for any fungus. (I tell visiting students to think of athlete's foot, which thrives in the microclimate of a sneaker. They get the picture.)

Diseases also attack grapes, to the detriment of flavor and sweetness. And late-season downy mildew can remove so many leaves that it slows a crop's maturity.

We're lucky to have a substantial workforce already in place when it's time to pick grapes. We all stop our other tasks and pick them together. We pick one variety at a time; white-wine grapes are first. We try to process each variety on the day of picking. First comes a trip through the destemmer-crusher, a magical machine that separates the grapes from the stem and then *slightly* crushes each grape, just enough to break the skin.

After destemming and crushing, grapes are tested for sweetness (a sugar measurement called brix) and acidity; adjustments to these qualities are made later.

White grapes go directly to the wine press. Our press cost $50,000 and holds two tons of grapes. It was purchased in the middle of harvest two years ago when our old press failed (big panic). It has an automated program that *gently* squeezes the juice from the grapes. The juice is pumped into a stainless-steel tank, yeast is added, and fermentation begins. The tanks are temperature controlled so that flavors and aromas aren't lost due to high fermentation temperatures; 55 degrees is best.

Red grapes take a different path. They go directly into the tank and are then fermented. Fermenting "on the skins" extracts the red color for a good-looking wine. Higher fermentation temperatures enhance the color. We press red grapes at the end of fermentation, separating skins and seeds from the wine.

As soon as we're done pressing grapes we clean and store the press for next year's harvest — our $50,000 investment sits idle 11 months.

Fermentation takes one to two weeks but can start slowly (more panic). We remove carbon dioxide, a byproduct of fermentation, by exhausting it to the outside via a separate piping system. It's important to keep air out of the tanks while the wine is maturing — oxygen in air oxidizes wine, killing flavor. After we've filled a tank we pump nitrogen into it to expel any remaining air.

Once in the tank, both reds and whites are kept at 55 degrees while going through a long process of settling, filtering, and clarifying. Because each variety is fermented separately, we blend the wines just before bottling. We begin bottling white wines after six months, reds after a year and a half (or longer).

Bottling is an exacting process. We use steam to sterilize our bottling machine. Filters remove bacteria and yeast before the wine goes into the bottle. (Yeast cells in the bottle can restart fermentation, with negative results. In my first year of wine making, I had to pay for the cleaning of a customer's rug when the cork blew off a bottle of our wine.) Finally, the cork, capsule, and label are applied, and the wine is ready to sell. It takes most of a day to bottle a run of 250 cases.

Wine making doesn't always go smoothly, but one way or another there's always something new to learn.

Planting Apple Trees (Again)

Spring is coming, and farmers, including this one, are starting to think about planting.

I am the 10th generation of my family to farm in this area. My grandfather, William Mount, was what was then called a general farmer. He grew several crops: potatoes, wheat, rye, corn, vegetables, and a few apples. Not nearly as many crops as the 45 we grow today at Terhune Orchards but enough to cover his marketing opportunities. His farm was on Route 1 in West Windsor, now the location of Canal Pointe condos. He grew apples on about five acres. His apples had names you don't hear much anymore — Ben Davis, Pippen, Greening, Nero, York, Jonathan, Rome Beauty, Paragon, Stayman, Transparent, Delicious — varieties that link today's apple farmers to a long and historic tradition of growing one of nature's great edible fruits.

My grandfather bought his trees from Steelman's Nurseries, about four miles south of our farm, on Quakerbridge Road in Clarksville, the location of today's Mercer Mall. As a boy I mostly remember Steelman's as the place where my mother purchased strawberries and asparagus for my brothers and me. Steelman's produced those crops for retail sale, but as a nursery it also sold plants and trees — strawberry, asparagus, peach, apple — to farmers. Many of the varieties it offered were jointly developed by Steelman's and Rutgers University, and by special arrangement a royalty on the sale of those varieties was paid to farmers' organizations such as the New Jersey Apple Institute, New Jersey Asparagus Council, and New Jersey Peach Council. When Steelman's went out of business the royalties ceased, but over the years the farmers' groups have used the funds received to establish endowments to underwrite agricultural research. I'm the current treasurer of two of these groups: the New Jersey State Horticultural Society, which this year awarded $16,000 in grants for research on apples and peaches; and the Small Fruit Council, which awarded $2,500 for a strawberry project. It's a cycle that continues down to the present, in which funds from the sale of trees and plants years ago underwrites research that makes us better farmers today. I am proud and happy to be part of that tradition.

When my grandfather brought home trees from Steelman's in his horse-drawn wagon, there were not, in today's terms, that many trees to plant. Five acres at 30 trees per acre made for 150 trees. "Setting out" was the process of lining up the rows, up and down, left and right, and on the diagonal. I can imagine my grandfather's uncle, Lewis C. Mount, from whom he purchased the farm, being on hand when he planted, perhaps helping as my uncle Russell Mount did when I planted my first trees at Terhune Orchards in

1978. I also imagine them planting the same way we did — with a shovel. Dig the hole, make sure the roots have enough room, and backfill with fine, loose soil so there are no air pockets to dry out the roots.

I love visiting other orchards and fruit-growing areas. There are so many ways to plant apple trees. I got the idea one year to dig the hole with a tractor-mounted auger — a lot easier than a shovel — but it didn't work out. The clay-loam soil on Cold Soil Road formed a clay pot around the roots, restricting drainage and eliminating root growth. Back to the shovel.

We now use a tractor-drawn planter. It opens a trench and packs the soil down, one row at a time. Our trees are planted three feet apart, so the tractor needs to drive slowly. Last month I visited western New York and saw a farm that used a two-row planter, 24 feet wide. It took a big tractor to haul it. I also saw a farm that used a single-bottom plow to make a furrow down the row. Trees were stood in the furrow and covered with dirt by hand.

Not all planting methods use a tractor. Three years ago, my daughter Reuwai and I visited a 400-acre farm in Washington State that had just been planted by hand. That was 1,200 trees per acre — 480,000 in all — by hand! Most times, trees are planted on a flat, level field, but in areas that might be a little wet the rows are mounded, with the tree row four to eight inches higher than the space between rows. We live on Cold Soil Road. Given that "cold" is a euphemism for "wet," we sometimes use this method.

The most unusual planting method I've encountered was on a fruit growers' trip to Poland and Germany. We visited a farm in the former East Germany whose owner was convinced his soil was bad. It was the only time I've ever seen trees planted without digging a hole first. He stood the tree on the ground and scraped the soil around it up to the trunk to cover the roots. He was puzzled that his trees weren't growing well. Being polite guests, we said nothing.

This year we're replacing 200 cherry trees that arrived severely damaged from the nursery last year. Most of them died, and the rest grew little during the year. We're also planting more Crimson Crisp, our new favorite apple. Some will replace a planting of

Jonamac, an apple that never caught on with customers. The rest will replace some failed grafts from three years ago when we tried to change over an Enterprise planting to Crimson Crisp. I'll try to have my children and grandchildren there when we plant. The cycle continues.

2020

THE BUZZ ABOUT BEES

There are so many words containing the four letters "buzz." Buzzword, buzz cut, buzzard, buzzer, and more. But the real "buzz" around Terhune Orchards, especially as spring approaches, is the honeybee.

This amazing insect is key to the whole cycle of fruit production. There would be no apples (or apple growers) without bees. An apple grows from an apple blossom, of course, but for this to happen, the blossom must first be fertilized by pollen from blossoms on a different tree. As a honeybee goes about its business — buzzing from one blossom to another collecting nectar, a food source for the hive — pollen attaches to its legs and body and is distributed to other blossoms throughout the orchard.

When Pam and I purchased Terhune Orchards in 1975, I knew I needed bees at bloom time. What I didn't know was that I needed a LOT of bees. I got bad advice when looking for my first beekeeper — I don't think that poor fellow's hives had more than a few hundred bees each. As I quickly learned, I needed hives with at least 30,000 bees. One or two hives per acre of apple trees does the job. The window of time for pollinating apple blooms is short — a few days. Some of those days, most likely, will be cold and rainy, so a farmer needs a large workforce of bees ready to pollinate when the weather turns nice. Bees will not leave their hives if it is cold or rainy.

Over the years I learned more about bees. I found new beekeepers to work with and now depend on Walt Wilson, whose bees are healthy, numerous, and hard working. He is also reliable; I depend on Walt even though I never see him. Beekeepers move their hives at night, after the bees have returned, which means Walt comes and goes at night. But when I need his bees, he brings his hives. When bloom is over and our trees need spraying, he removes the hives. We don't spray with bees around because we don't want to kill them.

From time to time I've tried other beekeepers, with mixed results. One year, the bees came from Florida. They arrived after bouncing from orchard to orchard on their way up the East Coast and were in an ornery mood — we still refer to them as those "ferocious man-eating bees." It was impossible to walk or work anywhere near those hives. Then, once bloom was over, the bee-keeper didn't return for his hives. He finally called late one night, saying that the blueberry bloom in Maine was early that year; he was up there delivering bees and suggested I move the hives myself. I did, and have never been stung so badly.

A hive needs moving at least three miles; otherwise the bees can become disoriented — rather than returning to the hive's new location they "make a beeline" to the old one. If there's no hive waiting, it can put them in a nasty mood. These bees were already nasty, and I didn't want to further rile them up. I convinced a farmer friend, Howard Myers, to "host" the bees at his place on Fackler Road, which as the crow (or bee) flies is about three miles from our place. The Florida beekeeper eventually picked up his hives at Howard's on his way home from Maine. All this was a long time ago, and per-haps it's safe for me now to ask Howard how he fared with those "ferocious man-eating bees."

Terhune Orchards grows apples on 50 acres. We now plant 1,200 trees per acre, making 60,000 trees. We would like to harvest 150 apples per tree. But the flowers don't all pollinate successfully, so we need at least 300 flowers pollinated per tree. Do the numbers: That's 18 million flowers. We rent about 50 hives with 30,000 bees each. That's 1.5 million bees to pollinate those 18 million flowers, so the bees really have to work. We also grow pears, cherries, blueber-ries, melons, squash, and other crops that depend on the same bees for pollination.

Farmers do many things to enhance pollination. I sometimes purchase pollen by the bag and place it in trays at the entrance to Walt's hives, so the bees have to walk through the pollen as they depart on their foraging rounds. I've used a leafblower to blow pollen into the trees and have purchased bumblebees to put out in the orchard to supplement the work of honeybees. (Bumblebees aren't nearly as efficient.)

Farmers can go to amazing lengths to pollinate their apple trees. A century ago, in the Aomori Prefecture of Japan, the growing system was very traditional. The trees were large, and pollination was done by hand, with 30 workers per tree on ladders, applying pollen with an artist's brush.

Pollinating methods continue to evolve. Recent research has focused on polymerizing pollen so it can be mixed with water and sprayed on blossoms. And a company in Washington State is adapting drones for pollinating fruit trees.

If we ever use drones on our trees at Terhune Orchards, I'll put my grandchildren in charge. Meanwhile, I'll keep working with Walt Wilson. I'll be calling him soon. Buzz.

COPING WITH COVID

None of us will ever forget the Covid-19 viral pandemic that burst upon the nation and the world in early 2020, upending our lives and the lives of millions.

Back in March, when the governors of New Jersey and other Northeastern states ordered "lock downs" that closed most businesses, stores, and schools and severely restricted travel, our chief concern at Terhune Orchards was keeping our families, employees, and customers safe. As a food retailer we were deemed an essential service and remained open, and all but two of our staff kept working. (The two who elected not to work did so out of concern for Covid; they later returned.) To keep everyone safe we followed the recommended protocols about sanitizing, mask wearing, handwashing, and social distancing. To keep fresh air flowing, we kept the doors of our public spaces open (much to the detriment of our heating bills in March and April).

As business owners, we were concerned about the survival of our enterprise. Would our customers continue supporting us, and would our sales be sufficient to keep us afloat? Sales in March, April, and May are slow under the best of circumstances, and we were surprised that they held their own — and then some — in the grim first months of the pandemic. It was immensely gratifying to see our customers respond in such a positive way as they followed the rules about masks, handwashing, and keeping six feet apart while waiting in line to enter the Farm Store, whose occupancy was limited to six at a time.

Meanwhile, we tried to make buying our produce as easy as possible. Within a couple of weeks of the pandemic we started no-contact pickup and delivery services — customers could place orders on our website or call them in by phone. Business was so brisk that we wound up asking our employees to work overtime, and we hired additional staff.

Another Covid-driven innovation was our weekend (Friday-Sunday) outdoor market, which started on the winery porch in the spring and moved to a big, airy tent for the summer and fall.

Wine tasting and wine sales moved from the winery into another tent, this one located by the big apple trees near the farm entrance. Tables under the tent were appropriately spaced, with seating at each limited to six people. One (understandable) innovation I didn't like was replacing our Terhune Orchards wine glasses with disposable (plastic) glasses. Whenever the pandemic is behind us we expect to go back to "real" glasses. The outdoor venue proved very popular, and we may continue it post-pandemic.

As the season progressed, it was business as usual in our fields and orchards. We planted and harvested, and customers flocked to our pick-your-own sites for asparagus, strawberries, cherries, and blueberries, all the while strictly observing the Covid protocols. We appreciated their cooperation.

As we moved into the fall season, usually our busiest time of year, the question remained: how to stay safe with so many customers pouring in, especially on weekends? Our pick-your-own apple business changed from sale by the pound, which is slow and crowds people close together at the checkout counter, to sale by the bag. Customers paid for their bag when they entered the orchard, and at the exit they just went on their way — no weighing and paying. If they wanted more apples, they bought another bag.

Another innovation introduced in the fall was online ticketing for weekend customers at our main farm (which includes the Farm Store and winery). To reduce crowding, we limited the number of tickets sold. After years of doing everything we could to attract more customers, it was strange to implement measures that did the opposite. It didn't help our balance sheet, either, but it accomplished our goal of providing a safer place.

I'm grateful to our friends at Rutgers Cooperative Extension for their advice on retail farm marketing during these extraordinary times. As I write this in late November, the pandemic is still with us, and will likely remain so through much of 2021. Pam, Reuwai, Tannwen, and I meet weekly to plan other new ways to meet the challenge.

TERHUNE STARS

There are many things that I like about being a farmer, but one of the best is the nice people who work for us. We would not be able to be here without them. The love of the farm that many customers express is often because of the staff and some are what I call Terhune Stars — they have been working here, putting up with us for more than 30 years.

I need to be careful of who gets written about first, but I will start with Elaine Madigan, who began working here almost 30 years ago, in September 1992. Elaine came to help at our fall festival and has never left. She has held the Farm Store together — taking on leadership, ordering, and organization. We are dependent on so many vendors; Elaine maintains a close relationship with many of them. New Farm Store staff are often overwhelmed with a variety of tasks; Elaine leads them. What needs to be done changes with the seasons, adding to the complexity; Elaine provides continuity.

As a naturalist and educator, Elaine has taken on a greater roll in educating and informing Terhune guests about the farm. She welcomes school tours and groups and leads them in discovering what family farming in New Jersey is all about. She has been leader and head counselor of our Terhune Farm Camp since its beginning. She has been leader in our "Read and Pick" and "Read and Explore" programs for preschool children and now, in the time of Covid, she has created a "Story Corner" weekly on our website. I'm not sure if Elaine knows how grateful we are that she is here. We like seeing her every day.

Other Terhune Stars are Gorgonio and Acela Martinez — husband and wife — known here as Emiliano and Margarita. Emiliano began in

Elaine Madigan

TANNWEN MOUNT

1990 and Margarita two years later. Emiliano is our most senior farm employee, responsible for much of the work that gets done on the farm. He makes all the cider, prunes many of the apple, pear, and peach trees, and plants and harvests many of the crops. As I noted in a recent column, when we plant apple trees, he is always the one who sits on the transplanter. Today, when my daughter Reuwai started planning this year's strawberry planting, it was Emiliano whom she asked to look at the fields with her.

Margarita has worked exclusively in our bakery/kitchen. Pies, cookies, chili, soup, apple bread and apples sauces, and above all *donuts*. And I mean a *lot* of donuts! I am continually amazed at the bakery's productivity when she is involved.

Emiliano and Margarita are truly amazing. They came to the U.S. and worked in California and Washington. They moved to New Jersey

146

TANNWEN MOUNT

Terhune stars Margarita and Emiliano Martinez

over 30 years ago and started working here at Terhune Orchards. They purchased their first home in our township near the farmers market and subsequently bought a duplex in Princeton. They now live in the house they bought next to our farm and recently they helped their daughter's family buy a house across the street.

Along the way, they decided they would like to become U.S. citizens. Emiliano told me that he wanted to vote. We had been sponsoring a weekly "English as a second language" class for our staff. It was quickly changed to a citizenship class. Both classes were taught by teachers we hired through the Princeton Y.W.C.A. Becoming a citizen requires passing a verbal examination and answering correctly 10 out of 100 possible questions that can be asked. It was a great day when Emiliano, Margarita, and their daughter passed on the first try.

We admire our Terhune Stars and are grateful they're with us!

THE GREAT EIGHT

I like New Jersey. I am proud to be a citizen of the state and I like living here. In one of his books, my favorite author, John McPhee, relates being asked once, "Why, when as a writer you could live anywhere, do you live in New Jersey?" His reply: "Are you kidding?"* My feelings exactly. McPhee goes on, paragraph after paragraph, to explain in detail why he likes New Jersey. My own reasons are not so erudite. I was born here, grew up here, went to school here, and most of all became a farmer here. I started farming in 1975, and joined a unique group — New Jersey farmers. Although New Jersey is one of the smallest and most densely populated states in the U.S., it leads the nation agriculturally in so many ways. It tops national production of about seven crops. Its ingenuity exceeds most of the other states in terms of agricultural research and innovation and breeding improved varieties.

When the state revised its constitution in 1947, it gave farmers a seat at the table of government. Most states classify farms as commerce and industry to be regulated and controlled by state bureaucrats. Few, if any, assign to farmers responsibility for agricultural policy and selecting the secretary of agriculture, a member of the governor's cabinet. In New Jersey, the governor may accept or reject the farmers' appointee, but the selection can only originate with the farmers. This is unique. For 50 years, I have traveled to many agricultural meetings and conventions across the country and have heard of nothing like it.

In New Jersey, the state board of agriculture has eight members, each serving a four-year term. Members are elected by farmers at the annual New Jersey Agricultural Convention. In 1982, when I was in my early 30s and still new to farming, I was nominated and then elected to the state board — up to that time, the youngest member ever. I was nominated by the Mercer County Board of Agriculture, whose president was Charles Bryan. I was thrilled to be nominated and am forever grateful for the opportunity it gave

---

* From John McPhee, *Silk Parachute*; Farrar, Straus & Giroux, 2010, p. 223. I am paraphrasing slightly.

me to serve, despite the commitment and possible sacrifice it might entail — Pam and I had no family backups (parents, uncles, aunts, grandparents) to help us in a pinch, and we were still struggling to get our seven-year-old farming enterprise on a firm financial footing. When I joined the board it was a culture shock all around — for me and the other members, all of whom were at least twice my age, in their 60s or 70s. Plus I had a beard, in those days not something seen on farmers' faces, at least in New Jersey. I didn't own a tie, and when Pam and our three young children drove to Drumthwacket, the governor's residence, for my swearing in, we had to stop on the way to buy one. I was also the only member of the board with a college degree, having graduated magna cum laude from Princeton with a B.S. in psychology.

I quickly learned that being a board member was all about participation, education, and leadership. I was happy to be a part; now, looking back on that experience four decades later, I've come to call the members of the board on which I first served the Great Eight.

The board annually recognized an outstanding young farmer in New Jersey, and I convinced the other members that we needed to interview prospective awardees at their farms. We visited parts of the state we had never seen and saw types of farming we did not know existed. Our small state's outstanding young farmers, men and women, have since gone on to compete and win in the National Young Farmer competition many times.

Shortly after I joined the board we were called upon to choose a new secretary of agriculture, as the existing secretary, Phillip Alampi, was retiring after 26 years in office. Choosing a new a secretary is a rare and significant enterprise — only seven people have served in the position in the 105 years since the first appointment, in 1916. Not being a political appointee, the secretary over time tends to serve many governors. The Great Eight learned to work together — my college education did not count for much, but our collective experience and judgment did.

I was stunned when the other members asked me to be a candidate for the job. It was tempting , but after many sleepless nights I realized how much I wanted to remain a full-time working farmer, and said no.

As we proceeded through the selection process I came to know the board as the finest individuals with whom I've ever worked. I remember Ray Blew of Cumberland County. Such a smart man, with such great judgment. My own judgment improved from interacting with my vastly more experienced peers — in particular Ray, Bob Dobbs, and Rod MacDougal. We ended up choosing as our new secretary Arthur (Art) Brown, who took seriously the idea of helping every farmer in the state and became one of the best ever in that position.

As a board, we visited the newly elected governor, Tom Kean, to press him on the need for promoting New Jersey agriculture. I remember showing him a coupon that a Virginia farmer had placed in a bushel of green beans sold at our Terhune Orchards store. The coupon, worth $10, was a simple and relatively inexpensive way of marketing Virginia's produce. I told the governor that New Jersey should invest in agricultural marketing, too. After we left the meeting, my fellow board members made sure I noticed that the governor kept the coupon. The governor was persuaded, and the end result was the longstanding and hugely successful "Jersey Fresh" program, which promotes the value of locally grown produce.

The board also worked on milk marketing (incredibly complicated and only understood by dairy farmers), and we helped pass a farm winery bill. The winery bill facilitated the growth of New Jersey vineyards and the selling of wine on site at the wineries. Little did I know that, 30 years later, Terhune Orchards would establish its own vineyard and winery.

The Great Eight's crowning achievement was the Farmland Preservation Program. New Jersey's farming land base was in rapid decline, and the program enabled the use of government funds to permanently preserve farmland through the purchase of conservation easements. This was a new idea back then; only a few states had such programs. Now, 40 years later, about $2 billion has been spent and over 240,000 acres preserved throughout the state. Voters approved the act establishing the program in a referendum. Farms on preserved land are prospering, to the benefit of the farmers and all New Jersey residents. Since Pam and I started our business in 1975, Terhune Orchards has grown from 55 to 250 acres, all of them preserved in perpetuity as farmland. Our two daughters are full business partners, and we expect the enterprise to continue long after we're gone.

With the passing of Ray Blew this year, I am now the last remaining member of the Great Eight. New members have taken their place, of course, and the board continues its work of choosing new secretaries (three in the last 39 years). Farming remains strong in New Jersey — "the Garden State" — and in no small measure because of this, our state remains a wonderful place to live.

* * * * * *

APPENDIX

Congressional Record, Volume 151 (2005), Part 15.

HONORING GARY MOUNT

HON. RUSH D. HOLT of New Jersey in the House of Representatives, Monday, September 19, 2005.

Mr. HOLT. Mr. Speaker, I rise today to honor Gary Mount on being named the 2005 Apple Grower of the Year by American/Western Fruit Grower magazine, sponsored by Cerexagri. This award recognizes the progressive approaches, hard work, and dedication to learning of a leading apple grower. New Jersey can be proud to have a native son singled out from among all the apple growers around the Nation.

Mount, a resident of Lawrenceville, New Jersey, has honed his growing skills along with his wife Pam, co-owner of Terhune Orchards in Princeton. Although Mount had grown up on his father's 300-acre apple farm, he did not originally plan on a farming career. Instead, Mount graduated from Princeton University with a degree in physiological psychology and had planned on pursing his Ph.D. It was only after his experience of joining the Peace Corps and serving in the Central Pacific islands of Micronesia that Mount decided to dedicate his life to farming.

For the past 30 years, Mount has continually pursued his quest to discover the best and most innovative farming techniques. Mount has demonstrated this commitment by attending industry meetings including serving as a member of the International Dwarf Fruit Tree Association, IDFTA for more than 25 years and on the board of directors for 11 years. Additionally, Mount has been treasurer of the New Jersey State Hort Society for about 12 years, former president of the New Jersey State Board of Agriculture, a New Jersey water commissioner for many years, and currently, a soil conservation district supervisor. Active also in New Jersey Farmland Preservation, Mount's efforts have helped growers pass on their land without fear of it being developed. Throughout his farming career, Mount has also considered it a top priority to have an environmentally sound approach to farming.

Particularly on pest management issues, Mount has worked with Extension agents from Rutgers University to develop an integrated pest management, IPM program at Terhune Orchards. By informing his neighbors about his approach to pest management, and then, creating a poster with specialists at Rutgers explaining the practices and benefits of IPM that is displayed at farm markets, Mount has developed a trusting relationship with consumers who feel confident that the fruit they purchase has not been fertilized with hazardous chemicals.

Mr. Speaker, on behalf of the entire 12th district of New Jersey, I ask you and my colleagues to join me in congratulating Gary Mount on his 2005 Apple Grower of the Year award.

* * *

From *American Fruit Grower*, August 1, 2005:

APPLE GROWER OF THE YEAR

Gary Mount's desire to seek out the best methods of growing and selling his fruit have guided him to the top of his industry.

By BRIAN SPARKS

SOMETIMES you can tell when a grower just seems to be doing things the right way. For example, Gary Mount's home state of New Jersey is hardly the nation's largest apple-producing state, and his acreage is about average for an East Coast fruit grower. Yet there's a very good reason he is *American/Western Fruit Grower*'s 2005 Apple Grower of the Year (sponsored by Cerexagri). His thirst for knowledge, whether he is experimenting with new technology, going to every industry meeting that he can (both local and international), or searching for the ideal relationship between grower and consumer, has allowed him to develop a successful fruit operation at Terhune Orchards in Princeton, N.J.

However, his path to reaching this level of success has taken a few turns.

He grew up on his father's 300-acre apple farm outside of Princeton, where he says he learned less about how to grow fruit and more how to work hard. But while he knew he wanted to be in farming at a young age, when the chance to attend Princeton

University came calling, his father insisted on it. As it turns out, his father was right. "Going to college, that helped me learn how to learn," says Mount. And not only has he kept on learning since then, he's also passed this important trait on to his children and the employees at his orchard. "The aspect of learning how to learn is one of the most necessary ingredients here," he says.

FROM BOOKS TO BUSHELS

Upon graduating magna cum laude from Princeton in 1966 with a degree in physiological psychology, Mount was set to pursue his Ph.D. But then his father died, and he returned home to the family farm to help finish out the apple season (it was also about this time he married his high school sweetheart Pam). A year later, inspired by President John F. Kennedy's call to service, they joined the Peace Corps and served in the Central Pacific islands of Micronesia.

"This was probably the watershed experience of our lives, and after returning home, we began to look at things a little differently," Mount remembers. Suddenly the idea of being a college professor, or enduring a daily commute to New York City, wasn't so appealing.

Gary and Pam purchased Terhune Orchards from its original owner in 1975 (the name was not changed partly because of local name recognition, but also because, quite frankly, high financing charges meant the Mounts needed to keep every last customer they had). This decision to go back to farming has not only allowed Gary and Pam to spend more time with their children, but it has also given them the chance to work side by side.

At the time, all of the trees were standard, but this soon changed with the planting of trellised trees, freestanding trees with stakes, and most recently, slender-spindle training systems. This latter technique helped Mount reach one of his main goals: early production. "I learned early on that to shorten the pre-productive period was one of the most profitable things I could do," he says.

KNOWLEDGE IS POWER

Mount's love of knowledge and learning is mostly satiated by his interest in technology and coming up with new approaches to doing business. "A new idea is the best tonic for being interested in what you do," says Mount. It has certainly helped, because Mount says he's never bored working in the orchard. "The information for solving farming problems is available — the key for me is finding it," he says.

One of the best ways to come up with new ideas, according to Mount, is by attending industry meetings. He's been a member of the International Dwarf Fruit Tree Association (IDFTA) for more than 25 years, including serving on the board of directors for 11 years, and has been to several of IDFTA's meetings and tours. He is also the current chair of IDFTA's Rootstock Research Committee.

Closer to home, Mount has worked with Extension agents from Rutgers University on pest management issues, particularly in the field of integrated pest management (IPM). "We had employed a private IPM consultant, and since then Rutgers has started its own IPM program, which has been our main help in fruit growing," Mount says.

Not only has IPM benefited Terhune Orchards on the production side, it's also helped to improve relationships with its customers. "Most of our customers are smart enough to know that there has to be some control of disease and insects," says Mount. "What they really want to know is that you're knowledgeable about it and are doing the best you can with the least amount of chemicals."

When the Mounts purchased a 65-acre orchard in 2003 (they now own a total of 185 acres), they invited each of their surrounding neighbors over for refreshments, and informed them about their entire pest management program. In addition, Mount worked with IPM specialists at Rutgers on the creation of a poster explaining the practices and benefits of IPM that can be displayed at farm markets. "IPM has been important not only as a growing tool, but also as a marketing tool," he says.

KNOW YOUR BUYERS

The other factor in Mount's approach to running an orchard is a commitment to direct marketing. Mount says fruit growers need to get in closer contact with their customers, promoting the fact that they have a product that is not only healthful, but is "really good to eat." This self-promotion is important not only with consumers, but with wholesalers as well. "A farmer that is promoting his own product is a tremendously powerful entity," says Mount.

For example, Mount points out that during the Alar scare of the early 1990s, "we sold more apples than ever."* The difference for them, and for other direct marketers, was that their customers knew all about their operation and felt confident in the fruit they were providing.

Mount admits that this idea is easy to say, but not always easy to carry out. Fortunately, he's benefited from being located in the most densely populated area of the U.S., with millions of potential customers within a 100-mile radius. At their own farm market, Stayman Winesap is the most popular apple variety, but the key is the multitude of fruits and vegetables available for purchase. "Variety is the spice of life for retail farm marketers," says Mount. In fact, Mount's business model is to sell everything retail. "If we have to sell something wholesale, then we've fallen down on the job." This presents the obvious challenge of balancing production with what can be sold at the market, and recently Terhune Orchards has turned to local farmers' markets and tailgate markets.

Another factor in Terhune Orchards' marketing efforts is its newsletter. Rather than relying solely on newspaper ads, the Mounts supplement their ads by mailing out their own newsletter and inserting it in the local newspapers. The costs of printing, mailing, and inserting are minimal, and the newsletter can also be sent electronically. The orchard's Web site, www.terhuneorchards.com, also adds to its marketing efforts.

AN EQUAL PARTNERSHIP

Gary and Pam Mount are not only life partners, they're also partners in business. Gary is responsible for the production and business management at Terhune Orchards, and Pam is responsible for retail marketing.

"That's how we started, and we still do it that way," says Gary. Yet there is another important part of Pam's life, and it's outside the orchard. She is very involved in the local community. She's served on the Lawrence Township, N.J., town council for seven years, and is in her second term as Mayor. The Mounts are also active in giving

---

* Alar (daminozide) is a plant growth regulator widely used by fruit growers until banned by the E.P.A. in 1989 as a carcinogen. A report on alar on *60 Minutes* led to widespread alarm about the "danger" of eating apples.

back to the community, something their customers are aware of and appreciate. For example, New Jersey's Farmers Against Hunger program was started in one of the Mount's barns. "It's a two-way street," says Mount, "and our town is supportive of us as well."

While both Pam and Gary Mount are busy at all hours, they've never lost the love of being able to work side by side. "It's a decision we've never regretted," says Gary. As they like to put it, farming and retail is a mix of science and art; Gary is the science part of the equation, and Pam is the art.

HIGHER LEARNING

Because it's not located in a major agricultural area, the labor supply for Terhune Orchards is slim. As a result, they need to be able to keep their employees happy and busy throughout the year. Growing a wide range of varieties has created a large harvesting window, helping to improve efficiency with limited resources. But there's something else that's been a hugely positive influence on keeping employees happy.

In recent years, Terhune Orchards has attracted more Hispanic employees who want to incorporate themselves into the American way of life, yet must overcome the language barrier. To alleviate this problem, Gary and Pam Mount hired a language teacher and began offering English classes every Tuesday afternoon. These classes have been hugely successful, both for the employees and for the Mounts. A couple years ago, the Mounts considered stopping the classes, until their employees changed their minds for them. "When they learn English, they can do more, and you can afford to pay them more," says Gary Mount. It's also helped the Mounts retain their employees by giving them a sense of belonging and pride in the work they do.

ACTIVE ROLES

Aside from his IDFTA involvement, Mount has been treasurer of the New Jersey State Horticultural Society for about 12 years. "It's my feeling that farmers need to work together in all issues, and the Hort Society is part of that," Mount says. He's a former president of the New Jersey State Board of Agriculture, he was a New Jersey water commissioner for many years, and he's currently a soil conservation district supervisor. He has also been highly involved with New Jersey Farmland Preservation, a unique program in which the state pays farmers to preserve their land. With land values soaring in the Garden State, the program has been a key to helping growers pass on their land without fear of it being developed.

Of course, there is life outside of fruit growing. One of Mount's passions is rowing, a love he first developed at Princeton and has maintained ever since. But for Gary Mount, his biggest joy is seeing his children grow up on the farm. "Farmers always tell you their children are their best crop, and we're no different," he says. Gary and Pam's oldest daughter, Reuwai, lives in Baltimore and teaches with her husband. This summer, they are spending a month living and working at the farm. The Mounts' other daughter, Tannwen, works full-time in the orchard and market, and is planning a new venture at Terhune Orchards — grape growing and winemaking. Their son, Mark, is in the Army's infantry division and is in the process of being deployed to Afghanistan. "He's real excited, and we're very proud of him," says Mount.

Growing with his kids, growing his mind, and growing apples. All three have given Mount great pride and led him to the top of his industry.

* * *

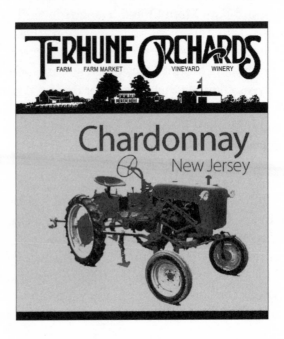